Poetry Handbook

For Readers and Writers

DINAH LIVINGSTONE

MACMILLAN

First published 1993 by
MACMILLAN PRESS LTD
Houndmills, Basingstoke, Hampshire RG21 6XS
and London
Companies and representatives
throughout the world

ISBN 0–333–54206–1 hardcover
ISBN 0–333–54207–X paperback

A catalogue record for this book is available
from the British Library.

10   9   8   7   6   5   4   3   2
03   02   01   00   99   98   97   96

Printed in Hong Kong

808.1
LIV

POETRY HANDBOOK

Dor

This book is dedicated to Camden Voices Poetry Group
and to poetry workshops and poets everywhere
fumbling, fretting and fighting
for appropriate forms of freedom
and a city of communion

Contents

Acknowledgements

I'd like to express my warmest thanks to the Department of Phonetics at University College, London, where I learnt phonetics with great enjoyment, and particularly to Dr Susan Ramsaran, my principal teacher, and Professor John Wells, who read the first three chapters of this book and gave me very useful help.

My warmest thanks also to the poet Julio Valle-Castillo for telling me a lot about Nicaraguan poetry.

The author and publishers wish to thank the following for permission to use copyright material.

Anvil Press Poetry Ltd. for extracts from 'Fête' and 'A la Santé' from *Apollinaire: Selected Poems*, translated and introduced by Oliver Bernard, 1986;

Anne Beresford for extracts from 'The Question' from *The Sale of the Morning*, Agenda Editions;

Carcanet Press Ltd. for an extract from 'Rubaiyat' from *In White Ink* by Mimi Khalvati;

Curbstone Press for extracts from 'Elvis' from *Flights of Victory* by Ernesto Cardenal, translated by Marc Zimmerman, and 'Nicaragua Water Fire' from *Eve's Rib* by Gioconda Belli, translated by Steven F. White;

Steve Duffy for an extract from 'Intelligence' from *Balloon*, Mattock Press;

Michael Hamburger for an extract from 'Death Fugue' from *Poems of Paul Celan*, translated by Michael Hamburger, Anvil Press, London, 1988;

Hearing Eye for extracts from 'Nawroz: The Kurdish New Year 21st March 1985', 'Is Love the Word?' and 'Daphne' from *Witness to Magic* by Kathleen McPhilemy, 1990;

David Higham Associates on behalf of the author for extracts from 'Titus and Berenice', 'Turnham Green' and 'Plato and the Waters of the Flood' from *Collected Poems* by John Heath-Stubbs;

Libby Houston for extracts from 'For the Record' and 'The Quarry' from *Necessity*;

John Lyons for extracts from 'Nicaragua Water Fire' by Giaconda Belli, translated by John Lyons, Greville Press;

Menard Press for extracts from 'Return' from *The Proper Blessing* by Arthur Jacobs;

New Directions Publishing Corporation for an extract from 'A la Santé' from *The Selected Writings of Guillame Apollinaire*, translated by Roger Shattuck. Copyright © 1971 by Roger Shattuck;

Penguin Books Ltd. for 'Swifts' from *Selected Poems: Philippe Jaccottet*, translated by Derek Mahon, Penguin Books, 1988. Poems copyright © Philippe Jaccottet, 1953, 1957, 1967, 1969, 1974, 1977, 1983. Selection, translation and introduction copyright © Derek Mahon, 1988;

Virago Press Ltd. for an extract from 'We New World Blacks' from *The Fat Black Woman's Poems* by Grace Nichols;

Every effort has been made to trace all the copyright holders, but if any have been inadvertently overlooked the publishers will be pleased to make the necessary arrangement at the first opportunity.

Introduction

What is poetry and who can write it? Keats says, 'Every man whose soul is not a clod hath visions and would speak if he had loved and been well nurtured in his mother tongue.' Likewise every woman. This is not another 'how to' book. Poets and would-be poets must do it themselves and take the consequences! But this little handbook does offer a view of poetry and give an account of some technical and general poetry matters which have proved useful, sometimes essential. These are all matters that have arisen in the course of our discussions at the Camden Voices poetry group, which this author has run since 1978. In this group we spend the first hour of each meeting discussing one or more poems by a different, usually contemporary, poet. The second hour is spent discussing members' own work. The Camden Voices group consists of a broad cross section of Londoners and over the past months they have all taken home this book, chapter by chapter, and come back with many useful criticisms and suggestions, for which I am most grateful. I particularly wanted to know if I had omitted topics someone would have liked included. I also wanted to be challenged if people disagreed with me and told whenever what I had written was unclear. I was.

There are countless poetry groups of all kinds in Britain today, meeting in pub upper-rooms, classsrooms, cafes, halls, houses . . . It is hoped the book may interest members of such groups or workshops, students, and also individual readers or writers not in a group or college.

The book is divided into six chapters and a conclusion. Although it can be read straight through, it can also be used for reference. Plenty of examples are given in each chapter. Among these examples I should like to apologise for sometimes quoting my own work. This is not, I hope, vanity, but because when illustrating a particular technical point I know what my intentions were if I wrote it myself, and secondly, because it does not need permission! In order not to multiply the notes at the end of chapters unduly, references are not always given for quotations from well-known works by poets not living today. Except for some poems with no punctuation, the modern typographical convention is adopted for both past and present poetry; capital letters at the beginning of lines occur only after full stops. This is both for the sake of consistency and because when poems or extracts from poems are used as technical examples, the additional capital letters might distract from the point being made.

The first chapter on 'Rhythm, Stress, Metre' introduces the fundamental rhythm of English, which is *stress-timing*. It does give an account of the traditional metres of English poetry so that readers may recognise them, but people beginning to write poetry are *not* recommended to start writing in traditional metres. The chapter also tries to deal with the much more difficult subject of what constitutes a good rhythm in contemporary free verse.

The second chapter on the 'Sounds of English' starts from the assumption that the primary material of poetry is the spoken word. This chapter has a section on phonetics, which many enjoy. However, it seems that some people are allergic to phonetics and so they would be well advised to skip this part. The chapter also points out various vowel and consonant patterns – rhymes, different kinds of near rhymes and so on – and discusses some of their effects when used in poetry. Again there is a strong caution against using thumping rhymes just because you may think this is what poems are supposed to have. The chapter tries to illustrate some of the subtler sound patterns used to good effect in contemporary poetry.

Chapter 3 on 'The Poem's Shape' begins with the line and goes on to the verse or stanza. It mentions some traditional stanza forms, and patterns using repetition of words or ideas. It moves on to forms for whole poems and discusses two traditional poem forms, the villanelle and the sonnet, by way of example. Again would-be poets are cautioned against strait-jacketing themselves in traditional forms but it is useful at least to be able to recognise them. The chapter goes on – via the 'verse paragraph' – to discuss form in contemporary poetry, why contemporary poetry often does not want a closed pattern and how each poem must find its own individual shape. What is required of this idiosyncratic shape and how does it relate to traditional forms?

What is poetry about? Chapter 4 is on 'Content'. It begins with poetry's primary requirements of economy and particularity. How does poetry convey ideas and feelings? What is poetry's scope? The chapter enters the current debate about this. Then it discusses allusion in poetry. It looks at words, asks what vocabulary is suitable for poetry, considers certain features of the English language. It looks at images, figurative language and lists some common poetic devices with examples.

What is poetry for? Who is poetry for? Chapter 5 is on 'Poetry in Society'. This looks briefly at examples of poetry in past societies, citing Milton and Blake. It gives a Somerset example of poetry's repercussions over nearly two centuries. It then looks at the state of poetry in Britain today and raises some questions. In the final section it looks at poetry in a very different society – revolutionary Nicaragua.

Is translation possible? Chapter 6 is on 'Translating Poetry'. It discusses the very considerable problems and gives some examples For the sake of continuity some of the examples pick up on poems by Nicaraguan poets mentioned in the previous chapter, but there are also examples from French and German poems in translation and some comparisons are made. I apologise that the examples are confined to languages spoken in Europe (though many of the poems were not written in Europe). This is not due to eurocentrism but my ignorance of more exotic languages, a state of affairs I long to correct.

The 'Conclusion' ends on a practical note and suggests where the would-be hearer, reader, performer or writer might go or look for poetry. At the end of the book there is a short list of addresses and publications, and an index.

1
Rhythm, Stress, Metre

'Poetry is ordinary language heightened', says Hopkins. It is heightened by intensity of feeling and meaning, concentrated into an economical shape. A successful poem is like an organic body, a body of language in which words interact with one another to produce an intense life.

RHYTHM

One fundamental way of heightening the language of poetry may be compared to the heartbeat in our own body. Rhythm. Perhaps our sensitivity to rhythm and its power to excite, delight or disturb us come from the time when we were in our mother's womb. The mother's heartbeat varies according to what she is feeling and these rhythms are felt by the unborn child. Pregnant women may feel a hefty kick or somersault when their own hearts are beating rapidly with excitement. 'The babe leapt in my womb', said Elizabeth, the mother of John the Baptist, when she ran out to meet her cousin Mary, also pregnant, with Jesus.

We are born into a world that is full of rhythms, day and night, plant and animal life rhythms. We love to be rocked. Our own heart also beats to measure our time on earth and when it stops we die. Our body has its own rhythms we may or may not control, and many of the things we actively do – walking, sewing, hammering, sawing wood, dancing, brushing our hair, making love – only succeed or at least are more successful when they are rhythmical, in time. Our bodies also have periodic rhythms – daily, monthly – and we not only may feel differently at different times, but even see differently, or perhaps feel or avert to different things.

Abelard sings in his famous hymn about heaven 'O Quanta Qualia':

> Nec ineffabiles
> cessabunt jubili

quos decantabimus
et nos et angeli.

There'll be no ending
the unutterable praises
we and the angels
together shall sing.

The operative word is 'unutterable'. Angels have no bodies and are not in time. Therefore they cannot make or utter songs and poems like ours on earth. It is our rhythmical mortal bodies that not only give our poems poignancy and power over other human beings, but make song and poetry possible at all.

Before we are born we must hear many strange sounds – glugs and bumps and gurgles – but it is after we are born, that rhythm is more fully linked to melody and feeling, firstly perhaps, in our mother's voice – and we have all the elements of music. Wordless music can have great physical and spiritual power. Words can also act as 'pure music' when we do not understand them. We may be deeply moved by a song in a language we do not speak but horrified when we realise what the words mean. We were 'carried away'. Spoken poetry has its music too but the rhythm and melody consist of words which are meant to be understood. We may enjoy the sound but we cannot really say we appreciate a poem unless we know the language it is written in.

We understand many words in our own language but when we speak we add subtleties of meaning by our tone of voice. This intonation pattern is largely suppressed in singing (the music may offer compensations). But the speaking voice can convey nuances that singing cannot (and of course it is easier to understand complex language when it is spoken than when it is sung.) Hopkins even suggests: 'The intonations and inflections of the speaking voice may be able to produce effects more beautiful than the fixed pitches of music.'

STRESS

The rhythm of English words comes from their *stress pattern*. Words can be broken down into smaller segments called syllables and when we speak we pronounce certain syllables with more force or prominence than others. We call these syllables 'stressed' and the other, less prominent ones, 'unstressed'. If we are listening for a regular rhythmic pattern in a poem ('scanning' it), we may call the stressed syllable the 'beat' and the unstressed syllable(s) the 'offbeat'.

Word-Stress

Every English word of more than one syllable has a stress-pattern. In the way it is usually pronounced, one syllable is more prominent than the others. We call this word stress.

For example, when we pronounce the word 'believe', we stress the second syllable 'líeve' and not the first syllable. But when we pronounce the word 'crític', we stress the first syllable 'crít' and not the second. Or to take an example of three-syllabled words, we say 'forgétting', stressing the second syllable 'gét' but 'génerating', stressing the first syllable 'gén'.

Sometimes word-stress may change depending on whether the word is being used as a noun or a verb; for instance:

Noun: They signed the *cóntract*.
Verb: To *contráct* a marriage

In words of more than one syllable – polysyllabic words – we may hear a main stress and and another syllable pronounced with a force somewhere between that of the main stressed syllable and the unstressed ones. For example, the main stress in the word 'unbelíevable' is still on the syllable 'líev', as above.

But the first syllable 'un' is more prominent than the remaining two ('be' and 'able'.) This is sometimes called 'secondary stress'. So if we mark main stress with an acute and secondary stress with a 'grave' accent we can write: ùnbelíevable.

Sentence-Stress

When words are put into sentences, word-stress becomes subordinate to sentence-stress. We stress certain words or a polysyllabic word's stressable syllable(s) in order to help convey our meaning.

For example we can modify the meaning of the sentence 'I love you' according to which word we stress.

'I lóve you', with the stress on 'lóve', could be a passionate declaration or a disclaiming answer to the question 'Do you hate me?' 'Í love you', with the stress on 'I', may mean I love you even if no one else does. 'I love yóu', with the stress on yóu, means 'it is you I love, not anyone else.'

If a polysyllabic word bears sentence-stress, that stress will be on the syllable appropriate for its own word-stress pattern. In the sentence:

> He has been upsétting my arrángements

there are two stresses, both on polysyllabic words. But when these words are stressed in a sentence, the stress has to be on the syllable bearing the word's own word-stress. We cannot say 'upsettíng' with the stress on 'ing' or 'arrangeménts' with the stress on 'ments'.

We also note that the sentence stress tends go on the more important or 'vocabulary' words, in this case 'upsetting' and 'arrangements'. Grammatical or function words, for example in this case 'has', are often reduced – we can say 'he's – and more seldom bear sentence-stress – except when they are contradicting. For example:

> 'He hásn't forgótten my fíver?' 'Oh yes he hás!'

This is called contrastive stress.

Many function words are reduced to a form with the indefinite vowel we hear in the last syllable of 'butter'. In phonetics this is written /ə/ and called 'schwa'.
For example:

> for is reduced to fə : 'It's fə you'
> were is reduced to wə : 'We wə going'
> to is reduced to tə : 'Give it tə Peter'

Whether it occurs in a word like 'butter' or in one of these reduced forms schwa is *never* stressed.

Alternation and Degrees of Stress

When we talk about rhythm in poetry we are talking about sentence-stress, but individual word-stress patterns also operate when these particular words are stressed in the sentence. Some long words may have a main stress and a secondary stress. For example, 'ùnbelíevable' can have a secondary stress on 'ùn'; or 'àcadémic', where the main stress is on 'ém', can have a secondary stress on the first syllable 'àc'. Similar examples are 'Pìccadílly' and 'àfternóon. When the word 'academic' is stressed in a sentence and just one of its syllables is stressed, this will be the main stress 'em'.

But as in other natural rhythms, there is a certain tendency in the English language, especially in poetry, to alternate beat and offbeat, it is, therefore, quite likely that another syllable would also carry a beat and 'academic' or 'Piccadilly' would thus bear two stresses, making two beats. The first of these on the syllables 'ac' and 'Picc' respectively is the 'secondary stress' in the word. Some writers, such as G. S. Fraser in his *Metre, Rhyme and Free Verse*,[1] even distinguish four degrees of stress. We do not really need so many distinctions to analyse English rhythms. In speech we have quite a lot of choice about what we choose to stress in a sentence (and could analyse this indefinitely in any utterance) and other factors are also involved. For example in any 'meaning group' – a phrase or sentence – the syllable on which last major pitch change in the group occurs (called the 'nucleus') tends to stand out as the most prominent in the group, even though other syllables before it may also be stressed. So, in the sentence:

I want some ápples, péaches, péars and plúms please

'plums' sound more prominent than the other fruits in the list because it bears the last major pitch change in the sentence. It is more helpful to analyse this as the 'nucleus' rather than saying it has an extra 'degree of stress'. In poetry we need to be able to hear stressed and unstressed, beat and offbeat, and to be aware of the tendency to alternate them. The beat is always on one syllable at a time, whereas the offbeat consists of one or more unstressed syllables.

Silent Stress?

Some writers on rhythm believe that as well as having stresses on words, poems can have 'silent stresses' to mark rhythmical pauses as in music. The most common example they give is when four-beat lines are mixed with or alternate with three-beat lines. Then, these writers say, the three beat lines have a 'silent stress' at the end, as they would have a rest if they were sung. For example when we sing 'Three Blind Mice' there is a musical rest at the end of each three-beat line thus:

Thrée blínd míce. [´]	(3 + 1 rest)
Sée hów they rún. [´]	(3 + 1 rest)
They áll ran áfter the fármer's wífe,	(4)
who cút off their táils with a cárving knífe,	(4)
did you éver sée such a thíng in your lífe	(4)
as thrée blínd míce. [´]	(3 + 1 rest)

As we all know the tune of 'Three Blind Mice', when we chant it we usually give it the same pauses at the end of the three-beat lines as when we sing it. But in ordinary speech we are perfectly at liberty *not* to pause at the end of the three beat line.

Take another example, the ballad of 'Sir Patrick Spens', with its alternating four-beat and three-beat lines, thus:

Lóng lóng may the ládies stánd	(4)
with their góld cómbs in their háir	(3)
wáiting for their ówn déar lórds	(4)
but théy'll see thém no móre.	(3)

When we speak this poem we do *not* normally pause automatically after each three-beat line: *not* with their gold combs in their hair [PAUSE] . . . but they'll see them no more [PAUSE], as this would sound intolerably sing-song and artificial.

When we chant, we may make rhythmic pauses like rests in music, but when we speak in a normal speech rhythm, we usually do not. Therefore it is not helpful to speak of 'silent stresses' for scanning spoken poetry and we should simply count the stresses on the words we actually speak.

STRESS-TIMING AND SPRUNG RHYTHM

In creative tension with the tendency to alternate beat and offbeat, the most fundamental rule of rhythm in the English language is *stress-timing*. By this we mean that in a sentence the time between two stressed syllables is (or is perceived to be) the same, however many unstressed syllables come between them. For example if we are tapping a rhythm of two beats we do not have any problem keeping time as the syllables increase in the following:

Jáne hópes
Jáne belíeves
Jáne disagrées
Jáne becomes enráged

But if we were to say:

Jáne and Jím enjóy

we would break the two beat pattern by introducing a third beat on 'Jím'.

For a clear illustration of how unnatural syllable-timing, as opposed to stress-timing, sounds in English, ring up directory enquires (it will cost you!). First say a seven figure London number out loud in the normal way: 207 3230. Now listen to the dalek voice of directory enquiries stressing each digit equally: it does not sound like a person speaking English.

When two beats come next to each other we have a natural tendency to slow down and when there are many unstressed syllables between two beats we tend to speed up. This can be used to good effect, as for example in these lines already quoted from 'Sir Patrick Spens', in which their juxtaposition makes the first two words 'long, long' sound even longer:

Lóng/ lóng/ may the lá/dies stánd/	(4)
with their góld/ cómbs/ in their háir/	(3)
wáiting/ for their ówn/ déar/ lórds/	(4)
but théy'll/ see thém/ no móre./	(3)

These four lines ('quatrain') are in what we call 'ballad' metre. The lines have alternately four and three stressed beats. The unstressed syllables are distributed irregularly between the beats. Because the English ear perceives the timing between two stressed syllables as equal, lines with a regular pattern of stressed beats in them sound rhythmical in English, even when the number of unstressed syllables is not regular. This was the earliest rhythm in English poetry: to count the stressed beats in a line and disregard the unstressed syllables.

For example the Old English poem *Beowulf* has four stressed beats in a line, three of which alliterate (begin with the same sound, see Chapter 2). The monster Grendel's mother 'greedy and gloomy resolved to go / on a sorrowful journey to avenge her son's death':

> gífre ond gálg-mod gégan wólde
> sórh-fulne síð, súnu deoð wrécan.

In the medieval *Piers Plowman* (1377) we find the same rhythm. Christ challenges Lucifer at the gates of Hell:

> Thou art Dóctor of Déath, drínk that thou mádest!
> I that am Lórd of Lífe, lóve is my drínk,
> and for that drínk todáy I díed upon éarth.

Even with modern spelling and pronunciation (which alters the number of syllables) the rhythm persists. Most nursery rhymes and ballads also count the stresses only. In his preface to his poem 'Christabel' written in 1800, Coleridge says 'the metre of Christabel is not properly speaking irregular, though it may seem so from its being founded on a new principle: namely that of counting in each line the accents, not the syllables. Though the latter may vary from seven to twelve, yet in each line the accents will be found to be only four.' He is wrong that this is a new principle but he is right that a rhythm with a regular number of stressed beats ('accents') is 'not irregular' in spite of an irregular number of syllables.

> Húsh, béating héart of Chrístabel!
> Jésu, María, shíeld her wéll!
> She fólded her árms benéath her clóak,
> and stóle to the óther síde of the óak.

At the end of the nineteenth century Hopkins calls this rhythm, in which the stressed beats are counted but the unstressed syllables between them may vary, *Sprung Rhythm*. He defines it thus: 'Sprung Rhythm is measured by feet of from one to four syllables, regularly, and for particular effects any number of weak or slack syllables may be used. It has one stress, which falls on the only syllable, if there is only one...' He notes that it is 'the most natural . . . for it is the rhythm of common speech and written prose, when rhythm is perceived in them . . . found in nursery rhymes, weather saws and so on; because, however these may have been once made in running rhythm (i.e. metre; see below), the terminations having dropped off by the change of language, the stresses come together and so the rhythm is sprung.'[2]

> I am gáll, I am héartburn. Gód's most déep decrée
> bítter would have me táste: mý táste was mé.

STRESS-SYLLABLE METRE

Unlike English the French language is 'syllable-timed' rather than stress-timed. With the Norman conquest French began influencing English and gradually poets began to write in metres in which they counted syllables as well as stresses.

Although a native English ear seldom has much trouble in distinguishing one syllable from another in English words, syllables in English are not altogether stable, especially where diphthongs are concerned.[3] The word 'imagination' often used to be counted as six syllables: i/ma/gin/a/ti/on. Nowadays we would always pronounce the final two syllables as one: 'ʃon'. However, even today different speakers might pronounce the word 'valuable' as three or four syllables, the words 'realise', 'creosote', 'lenient', 'influence', 'prisoner', 'listening' as two or three syllables, and the words 'fire', 'power', 'towel' 'royal' as one or two syllables. Perhaps it is not easy to imagine a poem containing all the above words, but one thing about it is certain, you would have a hard time counting its syllables. This fluidity means that even when poets are intending to count syllables as well as stresses in their metre, they always have a certain leeway in their syllable counting and stress is *always* much more important for rhythm in English than syllables.

With the Renaissance and its interest in classical literature, English scholars and poets attempted to adapt the traditional classical metres to English poetry.

In Latin poetry the metre depends upon 'quantity', that is the alternation of long and short syllables. Obviously this is not suited to the English language, in which the syllable length does not determine the rhythm. So long and short syllables in Latin metres were translated as stressed and unstressed syllables in English – beat and offbeat.

Lines of poetry in Latin were divided into 'feet', with different names according to the arrangement of syllables. Adapted into English the long syllables became the stressed syllables or beat (marked with a ´ below) and the short syllables became unstressed syllables or offbeat (marked with a ˘ below). The types of 'foot' were as follows:

Rising feet beginning with an unstressed syllable (offbeat) and ending with a stressed syllable (beat):

    1.   iambic   (ŭndó)
    2.   anapestic   (ŭndĕrstánd)

Falling feet beginning with a stressed syllable (beat) and ending with an unstressed syllable (offbeat):

    3.   trochaic   (úndĕr)
    4.   dactylic   (ánĭmăl)

The iamb and the trochee each have two syllables (in reverse order) and are called 'duple' metres. The anapest and the dactyl each have three syllables (in reverse order) and are called 'triple' metres.

Because of the importance of stress in English, requiring that each foot should have one stress, there are two other Latin feet which are totally unsuited to English: the spondee consisting of two longs, and the pyrrhic consisting of two shorts.

Lines of poetry could be written in metres containing one or more of any of the above four types of foot:

Line lengths

      Monometer   one foot
      Dimeter   two feet
      Trimeter   three feet
      Tetrameter   four feet
      Pentameter   five feet
      Hexameter   six feet

Lines with more than six feet have been attempted but usually break down into shorter groups.

Although originally the most common rhythm in English is the four-stress line to be found in *Beowulf, Piers Plowman* and many nursery rhymes, hymns and ballads, from Chaucer's time onwards poets have also favoured the pentameter with five stresses, and in particular the iambic pentameter.

Iambic

For many centuries the iambic foot, particularly the iambic pentameter, has been much used in English poetry, particularly unrhymed or 'blank' verse.

Examples (Iambic Pentameter):

> Ănd mákes ŭs ráthĕr béar thŏse ílls wĕ háve
> thăn flý tŏ óthĕrs thát wĕ knów nŏt óf.

> Ĭs thís thĕ fáce thăt láunched ă thóusănd shíps?

Anapestic

This metre, with its two unstressed syllable offbeat to every stressed beat, sounds faster than the iambic. Sometimes it is associated with regular speed, such as galloping. (See below Rhythmic Association.)

Examples (Anapestic Tetrameter):

> Thĕ Ássýrĭan cāme dówn lĭke ă wólf ŏn thĕ fóld
> ănd hĭs cóhŏrts wĕre gléamĭng ĭn púrplĕ ănd góld.

> Ănd thĕ búrghĕrs all vótĕd bў cómmŏn cŏnsént
> twăs nŏ móre thăn hĭs dúe whŏ brŏught góod nĕws
> frŏm Ghént.

Trochaic

The trochee and dactyl are falling metres, that is, the beat comes first and is followed by the offbeat. We may sometimes feel this 'dying fall' has a mournful effect.

Example (Trochaic Tetrameter):

> Thén thĕy búrĭed Híăwáthă

Dactylic

The dactyl is a falling metre, like the trochee, but has a double offbeat (i.e. two unstressed syllables to every stressed beat), like the anapest but in reverse. We may feel the following example combines the fall and the double offbeat in an effect of 'weary galloping'.

Example (Dactylic Trimeter):

> Túrnĭng ănd gállŏpĭng wéarĭlў
> hómewărd wĕ róde thrŏugh thĕ wíldĕrnĕss.

Irregularities

The dominant metre is iambic in Shakespeare's lines:

> Wéarў/ wĭth tóil/ Ĭ háste/ mĕ tó/ mў béd/
> thĕ déar/ rĕpóse/ fŏr límbs/ wĭth trá/vĕl tíred/

In fact the second of the above two lines is a perfect iambic pentameter but in the first line the first foot /weary/ is not iambic but trochaic. This is very common in Shakespeare and other masters of iambic pentameter and is called inversion. (We may also note the irregularity in the fourth foot of this same line; that the stress on 'tó' does not sound quite natural.)

Here is another example of inversion in the first foot of a predominantly iambic line:

> Whý ĭs/ my verse so barren of new pride?

It is also not uncommon for iambic pentameters to have extra unstressed syllables slipped in in the middle of the line. In any case, as we mentioned, the syllable is not always fixed in English. The second example under 'Iambic' above – 'Is this the face that launched a thousand ships?' – is a line from Marlowe's *Dr Faustus*. In the line that follows it in the play: 'And burnt the topless towers of Ilium' we note that in the metre 'towers' is treated as a single syllable. Obviously it is also quite possible to pronounce this word as two syllables: tówĕrs. In this case we would get:

Ănd búrnt/ thĕ tóp/lĕss tów/ĕrs ŏf Íl/ĭ úm/

which would make the fourth foot an anapest. In the last word in this line 'Ilium' the natural stress is on the first syllable 'Il' but as this is the antepenultimate syllable, the final weak syllable 'um' also gets a stress.

We have the option of pronouncing 'towers' as one or two syllables but sometimes extra syllables less naturally compressed are slipped into a metre:

Tŏ féed/ ănd clóthe/ thĕe? Whý/ shŏuld thĕ póor/ bĕ flátt/ĕred

The fourth foot of the above line has two unstressed syllables before the stress on 'poor' and so this foot is an anapest. This slipping in of a different type of foot into a regular metre, as in the above examples, is called substitution.

However, it comes naturally to us in English to 'swallow' un-stressed syllables between stresses and, in the examples of sub-stitution which follow, we probably do not hear them very clearly in ordinary speech:

Cŏnfóund/ thĕ íg/nŏránt/ ănd ămáze/ ĭndéed/
thĕ vé/rỹ fá/cŭltíes/ ŏf éyes/ ănd éars/.

Here the fourth foot 'and amaze' is an anapest, but not a very obvious one. In the line:

thĕ ímm/ ĭnĕnt déath/ ŏf twén/tỹ thóu/sănd mén/

the second foot is an anapest but not a very obvious one. Variation at the end of the line is also common:

Ĭ cóme/ tŏ bú/rỹ Cáe/săr nót/ tŏ práise/hĭm.

Here we have an extra unstressed syllable at the end of the line and also in the line quoted above ending 'why should the poor be flattered?'

Now here is an example of substitution of a trochee (which of course does not introduce an extra syllable) in the fourth foot, which does in fact have a strong effect in Hamlet's praise of Horatio:

> Tŏ sóund/ whăt stóp/ shĕ pléase./ Gíve mĕ/ thăt mán/
> that is not passion's slave . . .

The classical metres only fit English poetry *approximately*. Most poets have taken liberties with extra unstressed syllables, which do not destroy the rhythm, whereas the introduction of an extra *stressed* beat makes a far greater difference. This is the obvious reason why a pure syllabic metre does not work in English. Some poets 'promote' unstressed syllables to stressed beats or 'demote' stressed syllables to unstressed offbeats. If they do too much violence to the language of natural English speech, the rhythm or the poem itself fails.

However as poets, at least from the sixteenth century onwards, have *intended* to write in these classical metres, it is worth becoming familiar with them and being able to hear them, even though they may not fit the English language precisely.

RISING AND FALLING

Iambic and anapestic metres are called rising because they end with a stressed beat. Trochaic and dactylic metres are called falling because the beat comes at the beginning and they 'die away' in an offbeat of one or more unstressed syllables. The effect is different – the rising rhythm is 'upbeat' and the falling rhythm 'downbeat'.

So it is a useful distinction even though one of the major problems of using classical names to describe English rhythms is that most poets writing in these metres use considerable free variation at the beginning and end of the line. Even in verse that is not regular, we can hear a rising or falling rhythm, which may depend less on a classical metre than on the syntax and quality of the words themselves. So, for example, rising rhythm would be:

He wóre the háng rópe on his néck

befóre the déed was dóne.

We hear the above lines as rising because of the natural word-grouping, bracketed over the lines. In contrast, here is a falling rhythm:

Answer écho answer

dying dying dying.

This example illustrates why a falling rhythm at the end of the line is also known as a dying fall.

The Foot and the Musical Bar

Some writers have compared the metric 'foot' in poetry to the bar in music. They are similar in that they mark a division of the sounds into equal periods of time. If we only allow English metres with one stress per foot, then as English is stress-timed, each foot will take the same time, just like the bar in music. However some writers suggest that, as in music, we should always put the stress or accent at the beginning of the foot or bar. Hopkins writes:[4]

> Every foot has one principal stress or accent, and this or the syllable it falls on may be called the Stress of the foot and the other part, the one or two unaccented syllables, the Slack. Feet (and the rhythms made out of them) in which the stress comes first are called Falling Feet and Falling Rhythms, feet and rhythm in which the slack comes first are called Rising Feet and Rhythms . . . These distinctions are real and true to nature; *but for purposes of scanning it is a great convenience to follow the example of music and take the stress always first, as the accent or the chief accent always comes first in a musical bar.*

The problem with this is that we lose the 'real and true to nature' distinction between a rising and a falling rhythm we hear when a line ends on a strong beat (which may be reinforced by a strong rhyme) or ends in a dying fall. In the three middle lines of 'Three Blind Mice' we hear a rising rhythm ending with a strong beat (and rhyme):

Thĕy áll/ răn áf/tĕr thĕ fárm/ĕr's wífe,/
whŏ cút/ ŏff thĕir táils/ wĭth ă cárv/ĭng knífe,/
dĭd yŏu év/ĕr sée/ sŭch ă thíng/ ĭn yŏur lífe/

When we hear the line endings (with rhymes) so strongly, it does
not seem appropriate to scan, as some do, with the stress at the
beginning of each foot like a musical bar, which means having to
run the lines on. We hear the strong rhymes wife/knife/life as rising
rhythmic climaxes and line-ends and we do *not* hear:

Thĕy/ áll răn/ áfter thĕ/ fármĕr's/ wífe whŏ/
cút ŏff thĕir/ táils wĭth ă/cárvĭng/ knífe dĭd yŏu/
évĕr/ sée sŭch ă/ thíng ĭn yŏur/ lífe ăs/

Putting the stressed beat at the beginning of the foot or bar does
not always match what we hear and loses the important distinction
between rising and falling rhythms. The concept of the musical bar
is useful to show stress-timing: the time between stress and stress
is or is perceived to be equal in English. But in poetry we do
not always hear the stressed beat at the beginning of the 'bar'
or 'foot'.

COUNTERPOINT RHYTHM

As sprung rhythm, which counts the stresses only, is 'natural' to
English, when a poet writes in a stress-syllable metre, perhaps
approximating to one of the above-mentioned classical metres,
often the classical metre – iambic pentameter, for example – is
counterpointed by a sprung rhythm.

Two rhythms are in some manner running at once and we have
something comparable to counterpoint in music, which is two or
more strains of tune going on together, and this is Counterpoint
Rhythm.[5]

For example, Milton's sonnet 'On his Blindness' is written in iambic
pentameter. Thus:

Whĕn Í/ cŏnsíd/ĕr hów/ mў líght/ ĭs spént,/
ĕre hálf/mў dáys/, ĭn thís/ dărk wórld/ ănd wíde,/

ănd thát/ ŏne tál/ĕnt thát/ ĭs déath/ tŏ híde/
lódged wĭth/ mĕ úse/lĕss, thóugh/ mў sóul/mŏre bént/

This is iambic pentameter, with a reversed foot (a trochee) substituted at the beginning of the fourth line. We hear this metre even though it does not fit perfectly on the natural rhythm of English. At the same time we hear a sprung rhythm, which has four, not five stresses per line, except that in line 2 we may give five stresses, but not on the same syllables as in the iambic metre. We hear both these rhythms at once. We could mark them thus, with the iambic pentameter above the line and the natural stresses of the sprung rhythm marked by bold:

Whĕn **I**/ cŏn**síd**/er hów/ mў **líght**/ ĭs **spént**,/
ĕre **hálf**/mў **dáys**/, ĭn thís/ **dărk wórld**/ ănd **wíde**,/
ănd thát/ **ŏne tál**/ĕnt thát/ ĭs **déath**/ tŏ híde/
lódged wĭth/ mĕ **úse**/lĕss, thóugh/ mў **sóul**/mŏre **bént**/

Another example of iambic pentameter counterpointed with a four-beat sprung rhythm comes in the second line onwards of Keats' 'St Agnes Eve'. Again we mark the iambic pentameter above the line and the four beat sprung rhythm and hear both at once:

Sť **Ág**/nĕs **Éve**/ ăh **bít**/tĕr chíll/ĭt **wás**!/
Thĕ **ówl**/ fŏr **áll**/ hĭs **féath**/ĕrs wás/ ă-**cóld**;/
thĕ **háre**/ lĭmped **trémb**/lĭng thróugh/ thĕ **fró**/zĕn **gráss**,/
ănd **sí**/lĕnt wás/ thĕ **flóck**/ ĭn **wóol**/lў **fóld**./

We notice how the iambic pentameter does not exactly fit the way we normally speak. These classical metres are *imposed* upon English. Nevertheless the iambic beat does establish a 'metric set' which we clearly hear and we also clearly hear it counterpointed by the sprung rhythm.

Yeats calls this 'metric set' a 'ghostly voice' and gives this example. 'If I repeat the first line of *Paradise Lost* so as to emphasise its five feet, I am among the folk singers: "Of mán's first dísobédience ánd the frúit", but speak it as I should I cross it with another emphasis, that of passionate prose: "Of mán's fírst disobédience and the frúit" . . . the folk song is still there, but a ghostly voice, an unvariable possibility.'

Here again, as Yeats notices, an iambic pentameter is counter-pointed by a four-beat sprung rhythm:

Of **mán's first** dísobédience ánd the **frúit**

Counterpointing creates a tension which can add greatly to the rhythmic energy and excitement.

PURE SYLLABIC METRE

A few poets, particularly in the USA, have attempted to write in a metre which counts the syllables but not the stresses. As English is stress-timed, these experiments are seldom successful except by accident. However it has been suggested that in US English the stressed syllables are less prominent and the unstressed syllables less slurred over than in English English. In other words there is a slight movement away from stress-timing towards a greater equality of syllables than in English English. Therefore perhaps the syllabic metres of a poet like Marianne Moore sound better in US English than they do here. This is for US English speakers to decide. I do not think pure syllabic metre works in the English spoken in England. The Japanese form, the haiku, with its seventeen syllables arranged in three lines (5-7-5), is not usually successful in English unless it has some support from stress.

QUANTITATIVE METRE

Attempts to write English poetry in a metre based on long and short syllables, as in Latin, are doomed by the violence they do to the English language. However, the sound of words, which includes the relative length or shortness of their syllables and vowels, does add to the music of poetry and this will be considered in Chapter 2.

RHYTHMIC REFRESHMENT

Poets today seldom write in classical metres, except for particular purposes, because these may now sound archaic, stale, pastiche. They may also sound unintentionally comic. If you write a love poem today, you do not want its recipient to give a bored shrug and ask, 'What book did you copy that from?' Neither do you want him or her to burst out laughing. So caution is needed. Good poetry gives a sense of freshness. Each age needs its own poetry and the best contemporary poetry can give us a unique feeling of excitement and sense of fulfilment. Most of the time contemporary poets write in 'free verse'. 'Free' should not mean the verse has no rhythm but that each poem has its own rhythm, which may be much more complex than a traditional metre. The worst contemporary poetry tends to be produced by the more bookish academic poets, because it lacks rhythmic energy, living contact with ordinary speech, and is *written* for the eye and the puzzle-solving mind, rather than the ear and the pulse. Some critics appear to be incapable of the most fundamental requirement for appreciating a poem: *listening*.

However, even for those who can listen (which is any speaker of the language willing to pay the necessary attention) and respond to a good rhythm in a contemporary poem which makes free of tradition, it is difficult to define exactly what a good rhythm is. Douglas Dunn has described free verse as 'the most crucial problem in contemporary poetry'.

One poetic quality that has been particularly prized in this century is *economy*, concentration. This applies to content, form, words and also to rhythm. We like our poetry to give a lot in a little. This is another reason why a traditional metre may sound boring in a contemporary poem, because we like the rhythm to be doing more than just one thing.

Rhythm is the poem's fundamental energy and if a horse is too tired you cannot make it win by flogging it. In the 1880s Hopkins may have been ahead of his time perhaps, but since the beginning of this century many poets have been exploring new ways with rhythm because they felt their predecessors, the Victorians, had worn the traditional metres out. All sorts of new ways have been tried but, as T. S. Eliot writes:[6]

There is one law of nature more powerful than any of these varying currents, or influences from abroad or from the past: the law that poetry must not stray too far from *the ordinary everyday language which we use and hear*. Whether poetry is accentual or syllabic, rhymed or rhymeless, formal or free, it cannot afford to lose its contact with the changing language of common intercourse . . . The music of poetry, then, must be a music latent in the common speech of its time. And that means also that it must be latent in the common speech of the poet's *place*.

Anyone who has heard Grace Nicholls read will know how much the rhythm of her native Guyana adds to this poem[7] in which she makes the same point as Eliot:

> The timbre
> in our voice
> betrays us
> however far
> we've been
>
> whatever tongue
> we speak
> the old ghost
> asserts itself
> in dusky echoes

FINDING A RHYTHM

You cannot create your 'own rhythm' in a vacuum. There is no such thing as a private language. You share your language with your fellow-speakers of it. You are not an Abelardian angel – pure spirit. It is your physical body that makes you both an individual and a member of the human species, a social being located in relation to others in a particular time and place. This is where you are at and the matrix of your own rhythm. You can only write for your own voice (even though you may not be a good performer; by all accounts Hopkins was not brilliant).

But having said this, how do you go about finding a rhythm for a poem? Firstly, it is interesting that three such different poets as Hopkins, Mayakovsky and T. S. Eliot all say that a poem's rhythm may come *before* the words.

Hopkins[8] on the composition of his 'Wreck of the Deutschland' (which is in sprung rhythm in a complicated verse pattern):

For seven years I wrote nothing but two or three little presen-tation pieces . . . But when in the winter of '75 the Deutschland was wrecked in the mouth of the Thames and five Franciscan nuns . . . were drowned, I was affected by the account and happening to say so to my rector he said he wished someone would write a poem on the subject. On this hint I set to work and, though my hand was out at first, produced one. *I had long had haunting my ear the echo of a new rhythm which now I realised on paper.*

Mayakovsky:[9]

I walk along, waving my arms and mumbling almost wordlessly, now shortening my steps so as not to interrupt my mumbling, now mumbling more rapidly in time with my steps. So the rhythm is trimmed and takes shape . . . gradually individual words begin to ease themselves free of this dull roar . . . Where this basic dull roar of a rhythm comes from is a mystery. In my case it's all kinds of repetitions in my mind of noises, rocking motions, or in fact of any phenomenon with which I can associate a sound. The sound of the sea, endlessly repeated can provide my rhythm . . . A poet must develop just this feeling for rhythm in himself, and not go learning up other people's measurements.

T. S. Eliot:

I think it might be possible for a poet to work too closely to musical analogies: the result might be an effect of artificiality; but I know that a poem, or a passage of a poem, may tend to realise itself first as a particular rhythm before it reaches expression in words, and that this rhythm may bring to birth the idea and the image; and I do not believe that this is an experience peculiar to myself.

It is sound advice to engage in some rhythmic activity – such as walking for Mayakovsky – when seeking a rhythm, as it can get you going more easily than slumping in a chair. Listen to rhythms from the world around you, the sea, the swing in the park, the revving up motor bike. Listen to the rhythms of your own body. *Watch* rhythms – athletes on television – and translate them into sound in your head. Listen consciously to the rhythm as well as the meaning of the language you hear spoken around you – the market caller, the bus conductor, the racing commentator. Wealth indeed! You also have an inheritance from the past: your mother tongue has been spoken for centuries. A contemporary poet needs living forms but you are the heir to all the English of the past, it has survived in you and it would be foolish to freeze all this wealth in the bank instead of using and enjoying your inheritance.

RHYTHMIC INHERITANCE

It is probably more difficult than it ever has been to be a good poet in English today. 'Free verse' does not mean no rhythm. It means refusing to be bound by traditonal rhythms, whose effect may be weakened by familiarity, and a quest for renewed rhythmic energy. A poet must find his or her own rhythm and voice (which consists of rhythm and the other elements that make up the poem). It is helpful to hear and read contemporary poets, listening for their voice and discovering what appeals to you and what alienates. It is also helpful to read poets from the past – out loud if possible – and listen to what they are doing. Some technical knowledge of matters discussed earlier in this chapter should help you *listen out* for certain things, or at least name what you hear. When acquaintance with rhythm, stress and metre becomes 'second nature' to you it can be fruitful in the difficult and delicate task of conceiving and gestating a new poem with all the rhythmic energy and complexity of a living body.

Contemporary poems, which are quite often short, *concentrate* a lot in a little and this gives them their power. This applies to all the poem's elements, including rhythm. We may become bored with just one simple rhythm, like a reggae player who always only plays the regular bass rhythm. We do not have to jettison this simple rhythm but can also combine it with all sorts of complex tunes. Eliot makes one suggestion:

> The ghost of some simple metre should lurk behind the arras in even the 'freest' verse; to advance menacingly as we doze and withdraw as we rouse.

We are not bound by his 'should' but note that he practises what he preaches, for example in this passage from *The Waste Land* the 'ghost' of an iambic pentameter pops in and out. He establishes a 'metric set' and takes conscious liberties with it:

> Under the brown fog of a winter dawn,
> a crowd flowed over London Bridge, so many,

I had not thought death had undone so many.
Sighs short and infrequent were exhaled,
and each man fixed his eyes before his feet.

G. S. Fraser defines 'free verse' like this:

> What I recognise as good free verse is verse which does not scan
> regularly but seems always on the verge of scanning regularly;
> which is neither strictly pure stress metre, nor stress-syllable
> metre, [nor quantitative metre, nor pure syllabics], but which
> often seems to be getting near to one or other of these, perhaps
> attempting to fuse two of them, perhaps deliberately alternating
> between one and another.

We can establish a metric set, like Eliot's 'ghost of an iambic
pentameter'. We can counterpoint it, say by a four-beat sprung
rhythm and then play about with both. We can establish an
association with a particular metre, which can be oblique or ironic
rather than straight. 'There are many other things to be spoken of
besides "the murmur of innumerable bees" [n.b. this is an iambic
pentameter]. Dissonance, even cacophony has its place.'

We do not have to do any of these things . We are free to try any
way we please to produce rhythmic energy. But some elements
in the English language have a very long history and appear
fundamental to it. It is very unlikely that a poem will have rhythmic
power in English if it disregards all the following three points.

1. STRESS-TIMING.
2. ALTERNATION: the tendency to alternate between beat and
   offbeat. Different rhythmic effects created by irregular (as
   in sprung rhythm) or regular (single, double etc) offbeats or
   mixtures. Note that (1) and (2) are complementary and also in
   tension.
3. RISING AND FALLING RHYTHMS: the different effects of rising
   [offbeat + beat] and falling [beat + offbeat] rhythms.

RHYTHMIC ASSOCIATION

When we establish a metric set with a particularly insistent metre,
we may set up a rhythmic association with famous poems in that

metre. For example, if we write several lines (particularly if we write four) in anapestic tetrameter:

$$\breve{}\breve{}\prime/\breve{}\breve{}\prime/\breve{}\breve{}\prime/\breve{}\breve{}\prime/$$

we 'set' the rhythm of Byron's 'Destruction of Sennacherib': 'The Assyrian came down like a wolf on the fold.' Everyone familiar with Byron's famous poem will have it somewhere at the back of their mind on reading verses[10] such as:

> Now the negative forces are clever and bold
> flaunting their victory for all to behold.
> They appeal to the worst in us, hate, fear and greed
> and the state of this country is bitter indeed.

After reading more of these verses about the ill effects of Thatcherism on this country, perhaps the association 'Destruction' will come to mind.

When discussing the traditional metres above, we suggested that the anapest may be associated with galloping. We should be cautious of making such comparisons. There are many ways in which a human voice reciting a poem in anapestic tetrameter does *not* sound like a horse galloping. It is simply a metre that we *may associate* with galloping, partly because we are familiar with poems in our language where it has been so associated. Likewise falling rhythms do not have to sound melancholy. It is simply that they have a certain quality which poets in our language have exploited for melancholy effects and thus built up an association – by no means constant – in our tradition. The way in which a particular rhythm evokes a rhythm in the world or conveys a feeling is much more complex and delicate than simple imitation.

Here are some examples of the use of rhythm in contemporary poetry. We can look at them here but there are three points to remember as we do so:

1. Rhythm does not operate in isolation. Poems consist of words, which as well as rhythm, have sound, meaning, associations and so on and rhythmic subtleties work together with all of these to create a poem's complex economy.
2. The examples below are necessarily excerpts from poems but a poem's rhythmic structure may only become fully apparent from the whole poem (or section of a long poem).

3. Precisely because the rhythms of contemporary verse may be
   subtle and complex, it is essential to listen to poems out loud
   as well as reading them on the page.

EXAMPLES

I

1 To fínd the wórds, transgréss what fríends expéct
2 We néed a lánguage as súbtle-sóur as téars
3 that stúng to sée the míners sént ahéad
4 deféated banner high, to léad the Lóndoners;
5 how chéap the chéer we gáve, as we resígned them
6 to the sád sáfe stórage of hístory.

This extract comes from the middle of a poem entitled 'Nawroz:
The Kurdish New Year, 21st March 1985'.[11] The poem has already
established an iambic pentameter metric set. Here lines 1 and 3
are iambic pentameters. Line 2 is a less perfect iambic pentameter,
particularly with the extra-syllable offbeat in the third foot with the
word 'as'. Is it fanciful to hear the hint of a sob at this stumble? A
less accomplished poet would have omitted the 'as' and produced
the more archaic and more regular line: 'We need a language
subtle-sour as tears.' Things begin to happen with the metre in
Line 4, which is an iambic pentameter but with an extra double
offbeat at the end; 'doners', introducing a falling rhythm. Line 5 has
the extra offbeat at the end on 'them' and as there is no natural stress
on 'we' in the fourth foot (it would have to be 'promoted' to a beat
in order for the line to be an iambic pentameter), here the iambic
pentameter metric set is gradually dominated by a four-beat sprung
rhythm, which persists into the last line. In this last line the three
(alliterated) strong stresses immediately following one another :
'sád, sáfe, stór' force the speaker to slow down and produce an
elegiac effect (reinforced by the dying fall of the previous two lines
and in this last line itself), a slow drum beat emerging in contrast
to the sing-song of the iambic pentameter metric set.

II

1 Néat, rígid, bléak, póunded,
2 how you húmbled and hóunded me hárd

3   with your húge héavy hámmer strókes,
4   dull thúd, dull thúd, you thúnder
5   on the thíck cóncrete óblong sláb
6   alóng the shábby hóuse front,
7   ontológical gáp between lódging and pávement.

These lines from the beginning of a poem entitled 'Camden Town Garden'[12] establish a sprung rhythm alternating four and three beats to the line. This, we recall, was the ballad rhythm of 'Sir Patrick Spens'. But the above lines are not separated into four-line verses (quatrains) and the offbeats are much more irregular than in the ballad. The above lines have something of the strenuous quality of the four-beat sprung rhythm in *Beowulf* and *Piers Plowman*, except that they alternate three and four beat lines and, apart from line 3, the first three stresses do not alliterate (i.e come on the same initial consonant: see Chapter 2). We also note that there are fewer syllables to the offbeat in the more 'energetic' lines, particularly lines 1, 3, 4. In contrast the most 'philosophical' line 7 consists of four anapests plus an extra offbeat.

III

Here are two verses from the beginning and the fifth and final verse of a poem called 'The Question' (the complete poem is quoted at the end of Chapter 2):[13]

1.1   He lóoked úp
1.2   his bóok stíll in his hánd,
1.3   that dázed expréssion
1.4   só well knówn
1.5   sáddened her.

2.1   But he díd look úp,
2.2   looked thróugh her
2.3   óut to the wíndow,
2.4   gárden, róbin pérched
2.5   on japónica – bríefly . . .

5.1   And slówly she wátched
5.2   his éyes move slówly báck
5.3   the bóok trémbling – bríefly –
5.4   in the héat.

Here we have a tension between rising and falling rhythms. Each verse begins with a rising rhythm (lines 1.1, 1.2, 2.1, 5.1, 5.2). Each verse then proceeds to falling rhythms: Lines 1.3 and 1.5 in verse 1, lines 2.2, 2.3, 2.5 in verse 2 and line 5.3 in verse 5. Line 1.4 in verse 1 and line 5.4 (the last line of the poem) are rising, line 2.4 in verse 2 is rising but naturally runs on to line 2.5 and the whole phrase 'perched on japonica' is falling. We begin to feel that the tension between the rising and falling rhythms reflects the tension in the poem: will *he* notice *her*? The rising rhythms tend to go with his self-containment and the falling rhythms with her discontent. All the *words* of more than one syllable have their own falling rhythms: expression, saddened, window, garden, robin, japonica, briefly, slowly, trembling. Both the adverbs in this list, 'briefly' and 'slowly' are repeated with a distinct rhythmic effect but also with the contrast that 'briefly' occurs each time at the end of a line and 'slowly' occurs in the middle of a rising line. Although the tension remains and the last line of the poem is a rising rhythm, closing an episode, we are left with a predominantly falling effect – *her* point of view.

IV

The poem 'Return'[14] asks: after a long time in the desert/ what is it that brings back poetry/ like water to the Negev? It concludes:

2.1 I dón't knów. Not vírtue
2.2 or debáuchery, or ány spécial hárdship
2.3 or súdden lóve.

3.1 I'd bétter, ányhow,
3.2 make the móst of it,
3.3 and sáy the próper bléssing
3.4 for súch occásions.

Here we have parallelism – with interesting variations – between the two short verses. Lines 2.1 and 3.1 each have six syllables with a pause after the first three. But line 2.1 has three stresses and line 3.1 only two as the poem speeds up (in the ratio of 2:3) to move to its conclusion. Line 2.2 is parallel to lines 3.2 and 3.3 taken together. 'Or debauchery' and 'make the most of it' each

have five syllables with a stress on the third. 'Or any special hardship' is also rhythmically parallel to 'and say the proper blessing':
seven syllables with stresses on syllables 2, 4, 6: that is, an initial
offbeat followed by three duple falling feet, prominent for their
regularity. But the latter phrase has a line to itself: And say the
proper blessing (3.3). Gently heralded by its rhythmic parallel 'or
any special hardship', which came in the middle of a list and was
only given a half line, line 3.3 – 'and say the proper blessing' – is
the crux of the poem (and indeed *The Proper Blessing* is the title of
the collection in which the poem occurs). After line 3.3 the last line
3.4 dies away and we note that its rhythm parallels the last line of
the previous verse (2.3) except that 2.3 ended with a rise on lóve,
whereas 3.4, ends the poem on a dying fall: occásions.

V

The following example[15] shows a rhythmic pattern extending over
several verses, which may not be immediately apparent. We can
only give two verses here.

1.1   The páin of lóve is térrible.
1.2   Cóasters slip in unséen
1.3   before the hóot of dáwn.
1.4   They wéigh against the knúckled píers,
1.5   óily wáter lísps at their sídes,
1.6   and séagulls éat the cáke.
1.7   The páin of lóve bítes like an éarly squáll.

2.1   The pléasure of lóve is térrible.
2.2   We untíe the wórld.
2.3   Bóokham, Égham and Dórking fíelds –
2.4   they are lísted with Bárbary.
2.5   Póppies snág the néarest córn,
2.6   the róoks whéel dówn.
2.7   The pléasure of lóve bítes like hárvest míce.

We hear the rhythmic parallelism between lines 1.1 and 2.1 – in
which only one word is changed, although the changed word is not
rhythmically identical: 'pain' in 1.1 is monosyllabic and 'pleasure'
in 2.1 has two syllables with a stress on the first. Lines 1.2 and 2.2
each have two stresses. The rhythm of lines 1.3 and 1.4 is reversed

in lines 2.3 and 2.4. (Lines 1.4 and 2.3 do not completely correspond; although they have a similar rhythmic feel to them, in fact line 1.4 has three stresses (although 'gainst' *could* be stressed) and line 2.3 has four stresses – however the stresses on the three town names listed in this line make these three stresses feel more important than the final stress on 'fields'.) The rest of the lines correspond: 1.5 with 2.5 (4 stresses each) 1.6 and 2.6 (3 stresses) and 1.7 and 2.7 (5 stresses). The parallelism is subtle because the rhythm is sprung. Only lines 1.4/2.3 and 1.5/2.5 have an equal number of syllables and in neither of these pairs are the stresses distributed identically. Nevertheless the rhythmic parallelism of the two verses emerges clearly and the 'the pain' of verse 1 and 'the pleasure' of verse 2 are thus both contrasted and closely associated.

VI

The final example is a short complete poem called 'Song'.[16]

1.1	Mistákes, héartache
1.2	unexpécted deféat
1.3	búrnt áll bláck
1.4	déad béat.
2.1	Fíre chárred the héath
2.2	déath dríed the héart.
2.3	They who háted this éarth
2.4	have déeply scárred.
3.1	Yet déeper the séed
3.2	lóve sheds its lífe.
3.3	Blóod stópped stóne déad.
3.4	Moist wármth unfurls léaf.
4.1	My hópe is réd pétal
4.2	héart béat.

In this poem a two-beat sprung rhythm is in tension (counterpoint) with a three-beat sprung rhythm trying to establish itself. At the beginning the two-beat rhythm is 'set' in lines 1.1 and 1.2 In Line 1.3 the two-beat rhythm is still 'set', but now we are tempted to stress 'áll', making three beats. Then line 1.4 firmly restores the two-beat

set with two monosyllabic beats. In verse 2 (lines 2.1 and 2.2) it is
the verbs which struggle to establish three-beat lines against the
set two beats. We would naturally stress 'charred' and 'dried' but
may be tempted to demote them to fit the two-beat set. Lines 2.3
and 2.4 re-establish the two-beat set. In verse 3, line 3.2 also has
a verb 'sheds' which puts in a (weaker) claim to be stressed, like
the verbs in 2.1 and 2.2. Line 3.3 takes the impulse to introduce
more beats even further, to four beats, but as four is divisible by
two, it also maintains the two-beat rhythm with less tension than
the three-beat lines. As this line 3.3 does establish four beats, it
is the slowest line in the poem, which accords with the sense of
'blood stopped stone dead'. The final line of verse three (3.4) which
continues a faint ghost of a claim to four beats, does not sustain this
claim and is firmly returned to two beats. The last verse consists of
two lines in which 4.1 defiantly flutters its three beats, leading to the
last line with its two strong monosyllabic beats echoing the rhythm
of 1.4 but with different effect, both because of the meaning of the
words and the intervening rhythmic tensions which it resolves.

NOTES

1.   G. S. Fraser, *Metre, Rhyme and Free Verse* (London: Methuen,
     1970). Fraser's words quoted later in the chapter are from
     this book.
2.   Author's Preface to *Poems of Gerard Manley Hopkins* (Oxford:
     Oxford University Press, 1948).
3.   On the question of syllables, 'compression' and various other
     continuous speech processes see *Longman Pronunciation Diction-
     ary* by J. C. Wells (Harlow: Longman, 1990).
4.   Hopkins, 'Preface' to *Poems*.
5.   Ibid.
6.   T. S. Eliot, essay 'The Music of Poetry' in *On Poetry and Poets*
     (London: Faber, 1957). The other quotations of Eliot's prose in
     this chapter are also from this essay.
7.   From 'We New World Blacks' by Grace Nicholls in *The Fat Black
     Woman's Poems* (London: Virago, 1984).
8.   Hopkins, Letter to R. W. Dixon 5 October 1878 in *Selected Prose*
     (Oxford: Oxford University Press, 1980).
9.   From Vladimir Mayakovsky, *How Verses are Made* (trans.
     G. M. Hyde, London: Cape, 1970)
10. From 'Glad Rags' by D. L. in *Keeping Heart. Poems 1967-89*
     (London: Katabasis, 1989).

11.   Example I is from 'Nawroz: The Kurdish New Year, 21st March 1985' by Kathleen McPhilemy in *Witness to Magic* (London: Hearing Eye, 1989).

12.   Example II is from 'Camden Town Garden' by D. L. in *Keeping Heart*.

13.   Example III is from 'The Question' by Anne Beresford in *The Sele of the Morning* (London: Agenda Editions, 1988).

14.   Example IV is from 'Return' by A. C. Jacobs in *The Proper Blessing* (London: Menard Press, 1976).

15.   Example V is from 'The Pain of Love' by Peter Campbell in *Camden Voices 1978-90* (London: Katabasis, 1990).

16.   Example VI is 'Song' by D. L. in *The Rialto* 19 (1991). This poem will be the epilogue to the second edition of *Keeping Heart*.

2
The Sounds of English

Poetry consists of words and words are made up of *sounds*. It cannot be emphasised strongly enough that the primary material of poetry is the *spoken* language. As Hopkins says, 'Poetry, the darling child of speech, of lips and spoken utterance, till it is spoken it is not performed, it does not perform, it is not itself.'

There are many varieties of spoken English and a good poet will make poems in his or her own particular voice. It is a very special pleasure, for example, to hear the poet Steve Duffy, who has a rather dolphin-like manner himself, perform his poem 'Intelligence'[1] in his Sunderland accent. Here is part of the poem:

> the fishmonger is selling dolphin
> a bright and joyful animal
> and I ask
> who can measure
> intelligence!
> intelligence!
>
> stand in a bucket
> and pick yourself up
> physician
> heal thyself
> intelligence!

Of course this does not mean that all poets are good at performing their own work or that some kinds of poetry, such as dramatic poetry, cannot be written *for* a different voice. Shakespeare's plays, for example, are written very recognisably *in* his voice but *for* the characters speaking in the play.

I must speak for myself in my own accent, which is known to phoneticians as RP ('Received Pronunciation'). The description of English speech sounds given here is a description of RP, because

32

that is what I speak, but this in no way intends to suggest that any other accent or dialect of English is not equally suitable for poetry. Only a very brief description of these sounds can be given here but there are plenty of books for anyone wanting to pursue this fascinating and addictive subject.[2]

VOWELS AND CONSONANTS

We are accustomed to divide the sounds of our language into vowels and consonants. Roughly speaking, we form vowels by vibrating the vocal cords and altering the shape of the resonating chamber by raising or lowering different parts of the tongue in our mouth. (Other factors such as lip-rounding also affect vowel quality.) In forming vowels the tongue is never raised higher than just below the point where the air coming out would produce friction. Above this point consonants are produced. Tongue, teeth, lips interrupt or restrict – and thus shape – the sounds we make when we emit air. This may be done without or with the vocal cords vibrating, giving us voiceless and voiced consonants.

Vowel sounds tend to occur in the middle of the syllable and consonants on either side of the vowel. A syllable in English consists of a vowel sound with up to three consonant sounds in front of it and up to four consonant sounds after it, which we may express thus: (CCC)V(CCCC) or C^{0-3} VC^{0-4}. The word 'strengths' has three consonant sounds before the vowel and three or four after it (/strɛŋθs/ or /strɛŋkθs/).

PHONEMES

Sounds in a language which are contrasted to make distinctions of meaning are called *phonemes*. In RP English Gimson and Ramsaran[3] distinguish twenty vowel phonemes (including diphthongs which are glides from one vowel to another). For example the vowel sounds in bat and but and bet are phonemes because they change the meaning of the word. There are twenty-four consonant phonemes. For example bat and rat mean different things so /b/ and /r/ are phonemes. One speaker may (sometimes) pronounce 'rat' with a 'rolled' /r/ and another without, and the meaning is the same. So 'unrolled /r/' or 'rolled /r/' are not contrasting phonemes but *realisations* of the same phoneme.

ENGLISH VOWELS

Vowels are formed by raising or lowering the back, centre or front of the tongue. Vowels with the tongue high (just below the point which would produce air friction) are called 'close' and vowels with the tongue low are called 'open'. If a doctor wants to look into your throat he may ask you to say 'aaah' (as in 'father') because this is the most open back vowel.

Here is a list of the English vowel sounds with words as examples. Note that [:] indicates 'long'. So we have five long and seven short vowels but with different qualities. After that comes a list of the eight English diphthongs, which are glides from one vowel sound to another.

Front Vowels

The following four vowels are formed by raising the front part of the tongue (not the tip) towards the hard palate. They are in order from close to open. Try the sequence and you will feel the front part of the tongue getting lower and lower.

    i: as in bead
    ɪ as in bid
    e as in bed
    æ as in bad

Central Vowels

    ɜ: as in heard
    ə as in second syllable of butter. This vowel is called 'schwa' and virtually never stressed.
    ʌ as in bud

    Note /ɜ:/ and /ə/ are both half-close vowels. The only difference is of length. The vowel /ʌ/ is half-open.

Back Vowels

The following vowels are formed by raising the back part of the tongue towards the soft palate (velum). They are also listed in order from close to open. Try this sequence too and you will feel the back part of the tongue getting lower and lower.

u: as in booed
ʊ as in hood
ɔ: as in board
ɒ as in hod
ɑ: as in bard

Diphthongs

1. eɪ as in hay
2. aɪ as in high
3. ɔɪ as in boy
4. əʊ as in go
5. aʊ as in how
6. ɪə as in peer
7. ɛə as in air
8. ʊə as in cruel

Diphthongs are vocalic glides usually regarded as forming one long syllable. But as we noted in the last chapter, the syllable is a very fluid item in English. We have no doubt that diphthongs numbered 1–5 occurring in words such as' boy' or 'day' are each one long syllable. But we sometimes hear the diphthongs numbered 6–8, which are the 'centring' diphthongs (i.e. gliding to the central vowel /ə/), as two syllables (usually because of the meaning of the word): e.g. 'seer' and 'sewer'. In this case we regard /sɪə/ as a reduced form of /si:ə/ and /sʊə/ as a reduced form of /su:ə/. Some pronounce 'sure' with the same diphthong as 'sewer': /ʃʊə/ and /sʊə/. (However they may feel that 'sure' is one syllable whereas 'sewer' is two.) Some pronounce 'sure' to rhyme with 'door' : /ʃɔ:/ and /dɔ:/ and of course have no doubt both are one syllable.

In the above list of diphthongs the first five can all add /ə/ forming a 'triphthong'. But again we often hear this as two syllables, as in the words 'player', 'higher', 'slower'. Or in a word like 'fire' the 'triphthong' faɪə may omit the central /ɪ/ and produce the diphthong /faə/. Likewise some pronounce the words 'payer' and 'pair' identically. Conservative (or 'Sloane') RP produces the monophthong /fa:/: 'Fire!'. The same sound is produced by the broadest cockney as a reduction of a different 'triphthong' /auə/ and the word 'flowers' (RP /flauəz/) is pronounced /fla:z/. A point that Professor Higgins in *Pygmalion* does not note!

Distinguishing Front and Back Vowels

It is of interest to poetry to know roughly where these vowels are formed and how they are related. In particular it is useful to know which are the front vowels and which are the back vowels. If a lot of front vowels come together, we hear a different effect – which English speakers sometimes describe in terms such as 'lighter' – than a series of back vowels. Compare: 'He sits neatly in bed weeping' with 'The hard godfather's rude laugh caused pure horror.'

Vowel Order

As well as front and back vowels it is also useful to know their *order* from open to close. For example a *list* with a sequence of vowels, predominantly *in order* – from back to front and closing – may have a more cumulative effect than a random sequence. Ernesto Cardenal's poem 'The US Congress Approves Contra Aid' [4] ends with a woman listing things destroyed or pillaged by the Contra in an attack. The first time I read my translation – at a demonstration outside the US Embassy – I kept the literal Spanish order: 'The coffee beans, their animals, cottages, everything.' This was later revised to: 'Coffee beans, cottages, animals, everything' : /kɒfɪ biːnz kɒtədʒɪz ænəməlz evrɪθɪŋ/. The effect on the audience became noticeably stronger. Of course the close front vowel in 'beans' is not in order but all the other stressed vowels and the final (unstressed) vowel in 'thing' are in order, from back to front and closing: /ɒ, ɒ, æ, e, ɪ/.

Vowel Length

We counted five long vowels: /iː/ (see), /ɜː/ (bird), /uː/ (food), /ɔː/ (chord), /ɑː/ (harm) and eight diphthongs: /eɪ/ (may), /aɪ/ (die) /ɔɪ/ (toil), /əʊ/ (flow), /aʊ/ (plough), /ɪə/ (deer) /ɛə/ (fair), /ʊə/ (gruel).

When, as is usually the case, diphthongs are regarded as a vocalic glide within one syllable, this syllable is always long. (But as we have noticed, the English syllable is unstable.) In Chapter 1 we said we cannot 'scan' English verse by 'quantity', that is by length. But the length of syllables does affect the sound of the poem.

Long vowels should probably be called 'longer'. It partly depends on what they are combined with. For example 'bit': /bɪt/ is always shorter than 'beat': /biːt/. But 'beat' in turn is shorter than 'bead': /biːd/ or 'bee': /biː/. Nevertheless a series of short vowels – 'put it in the bin, Tom' – will create a different effect from a series of long vowels and diphthongs: 'Days, weeks, they toiled, cried . . .' A stressed long vowel will have a particularly strong effect at the end of a line and even more so at the end of a verse or poem.

ENGLISH CONSONANTS

The twenty-four English consonants are formed by interrupting (stopping or restricting) the air coming out through the mouth or nose at different *places of articulation* in different ways or *manners of articulation*. Air can be interrupted anywhere from your glottis (to produce a glottal stop) to your lips.

Consonant Pairs

Most of the English consonants come in pairs, which are produced in the same manner at the same place of articulation but one without the vocal cords vibrating – the *voiceless* one – and one with the vocal cords vibrating – the *voiced* one. For example /p/ and /b/ are both formed by stopping the air when you close both lips together. But /p/ is voiceless, whereas /b/ is voiced.

Consonant Kinds

The five main manners of articulation in which the English conso-nants are produced are:

Stop:	the air is temporarily stopped and comes out with a little pop
Fricative:	the air is restricted so friction is produced

Nasal:	air comes out through the nose
Lateral:	air comes out over the side of the tongue
Semi-Vowel:	the tongue is just below the level that would produce friction.

Stops

Some consonants are formed by stopping the air completely at a certain point and then letting it 'explode'. The stopping point may be two lips closed (bi-labial): /p/, /b/; tongue on gum ('alveolar': /t/, /d/), back of tongue on soft palate ('velar': /k/, /g/). So these consonants are called stops.

Fricatives

Some consonants are produced by nearly stopping the air at a certain point and causing *friction*. You can hear the sound of the air escaping. In a voiceless fricative it can be a hiss as in /s/ or like the sound you hear when you turn on a gas cooker before you light it. Try exaggerating the word 'if'. In a voiced fricative the friction has more buzz: try pretending to be a racing car and say 'zoom zoom'.

Nasals

Consonants which emit the air through the nose are called nasals. These are /m/ /n/ and /ŋ/ (as in singing) in English. If you have a cold and the air cannot escape through your nose, you replace these nasals with the voiced stop consonant formed at the same place of articulation: /m/ becomes /b/; /n/ becomes /d/; /ŋ/ becomes /g/. So what you say may sound like 'I ab dot goig' for 'I am not going'.

Lateral

For the lateral consonant /l/ the air comes out over the side of the tongue. It comes out further back for the 'dark' /l/ used at the end of words ('duel', 'milk') than for the 'light' /l/ used at the begining ('light', 'lick').

Semi-Vowels

Consonants which just fail to produce friction are called 'app-roximants' or 'semi-vowels'. We can feel that the 'y' sound in 'yes' (this sound is written /j/ in phonetics) is just a bit closer than the /iː/ sound in tea. Try saying 'Tea, yes!' or 'See you!' (usually pronounced /siː jə/). Similarly we can feel that the

List of the Consonant Phonemes

VOICELESS	VOICED	PLACE OF ARTICULATION
STOPS:		
p as in pip	b as in bib	Bi-labial (close both lips)
t as in tit	d as in did	Alveolar (tongue on top gum-ridge)
k as in cock	g as in gig	Velar (back tongue on soft palate)
AFFRICATE:		
tʃ as in church	dʒ as in judge	Palato-alveolar
FRICATIVES:		
f as in foe	v as in view	Labio-dental (top teeth to bottom lip)
θ as in thigh	ð as in thy	Dental (tongue to top teeth)
s as in sigh	z as in zoo	Alveolar (tongue to top gum-ridge)
ʃ as in shoe	ʒ as in measure	Palato-alveolar (tongue to gum-ridge and hard palate)
	h as in he	Glottal
NASALS:		
	m as in me	Bi-labial
	n as in knee	Alveolar
	ŋ as in gong	Velar
LATERAL:		
	l as in lull	Alveolar
SEMI-VOWELS:		
	w as in way	Labial velar (i.e. lip-rounding plus tongue towards soft palate)
	r as in rose	Post-alveolar
	j as in yet	Palatal (tongue towards hard palate)

Note that the consonants /ʒ/ (as in measure) and /ŋ/ (as in singing) do not appear at the beginning of words in English. The affricate is a stop plus a fricative.

/w/ sound in 'wool' is just a bit closer than the /u:/ sound in 'ooze'. (Say 'zoo wool'.) The sound /r/ is usually an approximant or semi-vowel but is fricative in the combinations /tr/ and /dr/ as in train, drain.

List of Consonants
Most of these consonants make the sounds normally associated with these letters but some of them have special symbols. The list of the consonant phonemes on p. 39 has words as examples of their sounds. This list is useful for poetry because it sets out systematically what a native speaker hears and this naming makes us more aware of what we are hearing. It is worth knowing which consonants are produced at the same *place of articulation*. We can hear that the pair /p/, /b/ are both produced by closing the lips when we link the words 'top boy'. Likewise the velar stops in 'trick god'. When we pronounce the alveolar stops /t/, /d/ in 'hot dog', we often introduce a glottal stop instead of the first of the pair: /hɒ? dɒg/.

It is also worth knowing the consonants' *manner of articulation*. The voiceless stops /p/, /t/, /k/, for example in words like 'pop', 'tap' 'crack' have this 'stop' quality in common. In contrast, fricative consonants in words such as the 'fifth' 'thief', 'these', 'five', 'thrive' have their friction quality in common. A sub-group of fricatives are called 'sibilants': /s/ /z/, /ʃ/ /ʒ /, plus the affricate (= stop plus friction) pair /tʃ/ /dʒ/. The friction of the pair /s/ /z/ has a hissy sound. The friction of the other two pairs /ʃ/ /ʒ/ and /tʃ/ /dʒ/ has a hushy sound; for instance, 'false kiss' is hissy, whereas 'rush' or 'churchy' is hushy.

SOUND PATTERNS

We enjoy the sounds of our language in themselves. Poetry increases that enjoyment by using *sound patterns*. In the poem as a whole these sound patterns interact with rhythmic patterns on the one hand, and the whole complex meaning of the words on the other. We like a poem to be *concentrated, economical*, to do a lot in a little with no waste. The German word for making a poem is 'dichten', meaning to make thick or dense: 'condense'. As we saw in Chapter 1, rhythm is one element at work to increase what a poem does within its space, sound patterns are another. They can add shape and texture to a poem, heightening its pleasure. The poem's concentration is increased if rhythm, sound patterns and meaning are all interacting intensely. In fact we cannot 'get' the meaning of a poem apart from its rhythm and sound. In a successful poem every element works together to produce its total 'meaning', which we feel could not be expressed in any other way; it is untranslatable.

Here are the four main sound patterns used in English poetry. Of course these patterns can be combined, interwoven, alternated and so on to produce many more patterns than four. But these are the basic ingredients.

When we symbolise a syllable as CVC (consonant vowel consonant) C represents a consonant cluster of one or more consonants (and in English, as we saw, this can be 0–3 before the vowel and 0–4 after the vowel). In the list of sound patterns below the unvarying parts of the syllable are written in **bold** and underlined. Patterns 1 and 2 are consonant patterns (which both come under the umbrella term of 'consonance'), pattern 3 is a vowel pattern and pattern 4 uses both consonants and vowels. The first three patterns have only one element which remains the same (each a different one of the three available).

1. **C** V C   good/game   ALLITERATION ⎫
2. C V **C**   smile/well   CONSONANT RHYME ⎬ CONSONANCE
3. C **V** C   so/goat   ASSONANCE ⎭

Thus both alliteration and consonant rhyme are kinds of *consonance*. The third pattern with just one unchanging element is a vowel pattern, called *assonance*.

The fourth pattern has two elements which remain the same: vowel and final consonant:

4. C **V C**   send/mend   RHYME

To complete the permutations of two unvarying elements, we can also have alliteration-plus-assonance: great/grape; and alliteration-plus-consonant rhyme: big/bug (a kind of double consonance, which we may also call 'consonation'). Various names have been given to these combinations.

All these patterns are of course much more forceful when they occur on stressed syllables.

Consonant Patterns (Consonance)

The usual umbrella term to describe consonant patterns is 'consonance'. As a special, historically important, form of consonance, the name 'alliteration' is used for consonants repeated at the beginning of a word or syllable: for instance, 'Mother made more demands'. In Old English and medieval alliterative verse the alliteration *must* be on a stressed syllable. The name 'consonant rhyme' is is used for consonants repeated at the end of a word, most commonly at the end of a line:

> She sent me cream/ tasting of home.

Obviously if the consonant is repeated in the middle of a word you may have a certain choice as to whether it is at the end of one syllable or the beginning of another. The syllable division in crum/ble seems obvious but what about ye/llow or yell/ow? A line or passage may repeat the same consonants randomly at the beginning, middle and ends of words and this diffuse pattern is just called consonance; for example, 'The butcher had doubly snubbed the baker's job before the hubbub began'. Of course, this diffuse pattern of consonance may include alliteration: 'Go and get a bigger dog to begin the game'.

Alliteration
Alliteration is the sound pattern used in the earliest English poetry. *Beowulf* has lines with four stressed syllables, the first three of which alliterate.. Here is the example quoted in Chapter 1 with the alliteration in bold:

> **g**ífre ond **g**álg-mod **g**égan wólde
> **s**órh-fulne sıð, **s**únu deoð wrécan.

And here is a medieval example, also quoted in chapter 1:

> Thou art **D**óctor of **D**éath, **dr**ínk that thou mádest!
> I that am **L**órd of **L**ífe, **l**óve is my drínk,
> and for that **dr**ínk todáy I **d**íed upon éarth.

In this example, we note that the alliteration is with the second syllable of the word 'todáy' – 'dáy' – which is the stressed syllable in this word. In Old English alliterative verse alliteration has to be on a stressed monosyllabic word or stressed syllable. Stressed syllables beginning with any vowel (i.e. zero consonants) are counted as alliterating: 'Audrey owned up'.

Alliterative verse often has an energetic or heroic feel to it and this has been exploited by later poets, Hopkins in particular. Here is the beginning of the heavily alliterated 'Wreck of the Deutschland':

> Thou mastering me
> God! giver of breath and bread;
> world's strand, sway of the sea;
> lord of living and dead.

There may be less than complete alliteration as in the above: strand/sway/sea, where /s/ is constant but the other initial consonants combined with it vary.

As we noted above, most of the English consonants come in voiceless/voiced *pairs*. A sequence of stressed syllables containing consonants belonging to a pair may have the effect of near-alliteration:

> Betty put butter on the peas

> Five very fine veils

Note that the spelling 'th' represents *both* sounds of a voiceless/voiced pair: /θ/ /ð/. Then think those thoughts: /ðen θɪŋk ðɔz θɔ:ts/ is thus on the same pattern as the above two examples containing both voiced and voiceless consonants of a pair.

For its strongest effect alliteration must be on stressed syllables but we also find the weaker off stress alliteration:

> He remémbered the reply with reséntment.

Consonant Rhyme
Alliteration has the same consonant at the beginning of the word or syllable, consonant rhyme has the same consonant at the end of the word (and often the line). Many contemporary poets have used consonant rhyme when they want a sound parallelism more subtle than a strong rhyme. Wilfrid Owen made particularly effective use of consonant rhyme as here in the poem 'Futility'. We quote only the first four lines:

Move him into the sun –
gently its touch woke him once,
at home, whispering of fields unsown.
Always it woke him, even in France,

In his poem 'Strange Meeting' Owen uses alliteration-plus-consonant rhyme to produce its elegiac and echoey effect:

And by his smile I knew that sullen hall,
by his dead smile I knew we stood in Hell.
With a thousand pains that vision's face was grained;
yet no blood reached there from the upper ground,
and no guns thumped, or down the flues made moan.
'Strange friend,' I said, 'here is no cause to mourn . . .

Note that the so-called 'eye-rhymes' love/grove/move are in fact consonant rhymes because the vowel *sound* differs.

As with alliteration, we can have an effect of near consonant rhyme by the use of voiced/voiceless consonant pairs: enough/prove; ways/distress; dark/flag.

Vowel Patterns

Assonance

A repetition of the same vowel sound can 'colour' part of a poem with that vowel quality. We noted above that a sequence of back vowels will have a different effect from a sequence of front vowels. Each vowel has its own quality and a repetition of a particular vowel will permeate that part of the poem with this quality, as in the line:

the calm tarn of the far dark father

which is permeated with the open back long /ɑ:/ sound, whereas the line:

it gives me the pip

has a predominant half close short front /ɪ/. (See also below under sound association.)

At the ends of lines we may feel that assonance instead of a rhyme is slack and more suitable to pop songs, where obviously the final consonant is much less important than the final vowel sound that holds the note. Perhaps the following example is a little cruel:

> I could not say
> why he was so great.
> He was just my Dave.

Vowel plus Consonant Patterns

Rhyme
Rhyme has a different initial consonant but the same vowel and final consonant. Conventionally rhyme has often been used to mark the end of the line of verse (which also makes the poem easier to memorise). But rhyme is also used within the line (internal) and at the beginning of the line (initial). We will say more about *rhyme schemes* in Chapter 3.

Great caution must be used by the contemporary poet not to let end rhymes 'thump' or sound forced. If a rhyming pair includes an unusual word, the rhyme probably has a better chance of not sounding forced if the unusual word comes first. Thumping or forced rhymes can ruin a poem by sounding stale, clichéd or unintentionally comic. However, there are many ways in which rhyme, used with discretion, and with all the various resources of internal rhyme, near rhyme and so on can add to a poem's density and pleasure.

Full Rhyme
Rhymes can be on one stressed syllable, or on one stressed syllable plus the succeeding one or two unstressed syllables. One syllable on-stress rhymes used to be called 'masculine' (as they were felt to be stronger) and polysyllabic rhymes 'feminine' (as they were felt to be weaker). It seems unnecessary to pander to the masculine ego in this way so we shall not use the terms masculine and feminine to describe different kinds of rhyme.

One-syllable (on-stress) 'Strong' Rhyme: the strongest rhymes are of this kind: god/sod; man/can; come/dumb. Note that words like delíght/uptíght are one-syllable rhymes because the stress is on the second syllable. Apply/reply is not a rhyme of this type because the stressed syllable 'ply' is identical. The stressed syllable must begin with a *different consonant* as in reply/deny.

Two-syllable rhyme involves a stressed syllable and the unstressed syllable that comes after it: 'many/any; dying/sighing; doubted/ shouted. Rhymes of this type are sometimes used as a sort of diminutive as in: inzy/winzy; andy/pandy; itsy/bitsy/. Or as a sort of sneer, as in : hocus/pocus; mumbo/jumbo. When it does not mean gobblydegook, the rhyme mumbo/jumbo can also be an affectionate augmentative referring to a large mother.

Three-syllable rhyme includes a stressed syllable and two unstressed syllables following it: bicycle/icicle; greenery/scenery. Such rhymes are are often used in humorous verse.

Near Rhyme
There are various kinds of near-rhyme:

(a) *One of the rhyming syllables may be unstressed*: men/súdden; sét/léaflet. As the unstressed second syllable in both 'súdden' and 'léaflet' is reduced to schwa /ə/: /sʌdən/; /li:flət/, whereas the vowel in 'men' and 'set' is /e/, perhaps this should really be regarded as a form of consonant rhyme. A clearer example is: thing/eating.

(b) *A polysyllabic word may rhyme on its stressed syllable but not on the succeeding unstressed syllables*: lóver/shóvel; sýcamore/píck-me-up. This can, of course, also be described as a form of assonance.

(c) *Both the rhyming syllables are unstressed*: mánage/pórridge; lóving/góing. We note that the chiming effect of lov-ing/going: /ləvɪŋ / gəɪŋ/ is weaker than manage/porridge: /mænɪʤ/pɒrɪʤ/. This is because the vowels in the stressed syllable of mánage and pórridge – /æ/ and /ɒ/ – are both short and therefore more similar than the vowels in the stressed syllable of lóving and góing – /ʌ/ and /əʊ/ – the first of which is short and the second a diphthong.

(d) *Paired Consonants*: the effect noted above with alliteration and consonant rhyme produced by the use of voiceless/voiced consonant pairs also operates with rhyme. The effect is stronger because the vowel is the same. The pairs up/club; sat/dad; mice/wise; stuff/love have an effect that is close but not identical to rhyme.

SOUND ASSOCIATION

In Chapter 1 we discussed rhythmic association. We also associate sounds.

Onomatopoeia is a word whose sound illustrates its meaning: clump, screech, snuffle, for instance. However, even words for animal noises are different in different languages: only English cocks crow cock-a-doodle-doo. In Spain they crow 'Kikiriki'. A Japanese person once assured me that in Japan the noise made by bees is 'boom-boom'! Onomatopoeia is very seldom a perfect imitation of the sound it signifies. It is just that those particular sounds in our language are associated with what they mean. One of the most entertaining examples of onomatopoeia heard recently from a contemporary poet came in Linton Kwesi Johnson's poem about an alsatian dog who was sent to school with the Jesuits. Asked later to describe his schooldays, he replied with the one word: 'Rough!'

We noted above that English people often feel back vowels are 'heavy' or 'dark' and front vowels are 'lighter' in both senses. This is partly connected with the actual sound qualities but also with words we associate. For instance, we may have an association of flip with slip, flit, bit, little, trip etc. or connect a series all containing the central vowel /ʌ/ (plus final consonants /mp/): slump, lump, hump, frump, dump . . .

Or we may associate words all having the back vowel /ɔ:/ bore, yawn, jaw, more, floor, gnaw, hoary, caw, store. With consonants we may, for example, associate ideas like 'quick' and 'sharp' with the voiceless stops: snick, pop, snip, crack, tap, tip, slit. Or we may associate the 'hissing' sounds in the sibilant fricatives of 'this treacherous, slinky, slimy, slithery snake grassed.'

Vowels and consonants do not operate in isolation but together in actual words with meanings. The feelings we build up about words in our language have some physical basis in the actual sounds but are mostly dependent on a set of associations. In every case when we think of a group of like-sounding words we may associate, we can always think of plenty of exceptions.

We hear the sounds of English in words in sentences. We may be entertained by phonetic puns on posters and shop signs. It is very important for a hearer or maker of poetry to listen to *the sounds themselves*. It is one of life's great pleasures, in a city like London with all its marvellous variety of people, to walk about and listen to the sound of them talking, sometimes engaging in conversation yourself. Listen to the quality of their voices, listen to the sounds they make and their accents and dialects. Listen to the sound *patterns* and become more conscious of the countless ways in which speakers of the language use its sounds to reach each other. If you go about mumbling with a beatific smile on your face and people think you are daft, what does it matter if you are both doing your poetry homework and enjoying yourself?

EXAMPLES

We noted above that sound patterns do not work in isolation but together with rhythm and meaning, including all kinds of phonic association. However we shall try to give some examples of sound patterning here without giving a complete analysis, merely pointing certain things out.

First we return to some of the examples given at the end of Chapter 1 on rhythm.[5]

I

1   To find the words, transgress what friends expect.
2   We need a language as subtle-sour as tears
3   that stung to see the miners sent ahead
4   defeated banner high, to lead the Londoners:
5   how cheap the cheer we gave, as we resigned them
6   to the sad safe storage of history.

At the end of Chapter 1 we saw how the iambic pentameter 'set' in this passage gradually transformed itself into the four stress sprung rhythm of line 6. Now we can see how the build-up to line 6 is supported by alliteration from line 3 on. We noted above that alliteration is often used for 'heroic' effect. Here it is used elegiacally for the heroic 'defeated banners' of the miners. In line 3 we have the alliteration 'stung', 'see' 'sent'; line 4 ends 'to lead the Londoners' with alliterating /l/. In line 5 'cheap' and 'cheer' alliterate on the first two stresses of the line. Finally line 6 – in the four stress sprung rhythm of *Beowulf* and *Piers Plowman* – alliterates in exactly the Old English pattern: the first three stresses on 'sad', 'safe', 'storage' alliterate and the fourth stress does not.

In addition the /tS/ affricate of the alliterating 'cheap' and 'cheer' has an echo in the rhyme of its voiced pair /dJ/ at the end of 'language' and 'storage'. There is also the accumulating assonance of the /iː/ in 'need', 'see', 'defeated', 'lead', 'cheap' and of the /e / diphthong in 'gave' and 'safe', words which also have the near rhyme of the voiced/voiceless pair /v/, /f/.

II

1   Neat, rigid, bleak, pounded,
2   how you humbled and hounded me hard
3   with your huge heavy hammer strokes,
4   dull thud, dull thud, you thunder
5   on the thick concrete oblong slab
6   along the shabby house front,
7   ontological gap between lodging and pavement.

One strong effect here is the alliterated /h/ glottal fricative in lines 2 and 3: 'humbled', 'hounded' 'hard', 'huge', 'heavy', 'hammer'. There is alliterated /Q/ in line 4, carrying over to line 5: 'thud', 'thud', 'thunder', 'thick'. In the first three of these words the alliteration is supported by the assonance of the vowel /U/, which occurs in five of the six words in line 4. The total effect of lines 2–4 is energetic. Lines 1 and 2 have the internal rhyme 'pounded'/'hounded'. Lines 5–7 have the / / vowel assonance in 'concrete', 'oblong', 'along', 'ontological' and 'lodging' and /æ/ assonance in 'slab', 'shabby', 'gap'. The assonance of these two vowels alternates to form a series which is broken by the last word in the poem, 'pavement'. Thus: 'oblong slab', 'along shabby', 'ontological gap', 'lodging pavement'. The /e / diphthong in 'pavement' breaks the pattern and marks the end of this 'verse paragraph'. The end of the verse paragraph is also marked by the off-stress consonant rhyme of 'front' and 'pavement' at the end of lines 6 and 7 respectively.

The next three examples are all complete poems, extracts from two of which had their rhythm examined at the end of Chapter 1. One reason for looking at these complete poems is that the sounds in them are used not only to give the poem patterning and density but also to 'point ' it. Words with sounds in common may be connected by meaning or help the poem *progress* to its conclusion.

III

The Question

1.1.	He looked up
1.2.	his book still in his hand,
1.3.	that dazed expression
1.4.	so well known
1.5.	saddened her.
2.1.	But he did look up,
2.2.	looked through her
2.3.	out to the window,
2.4.	garden, robin perched
2.5.	on japonica – briefly.
3.1.	She spoke into the void
3.2.	of his mind – or hers –
3.3.	'Not again, never.'
3.4.	Nothing moved
3.5.	even outside nothing stirred.
4.1.	'Understand, I can't
4.2.	explain it more'.
4.3.	Again the silent afternoon
4.4.	the fear on her neck.
5.1.	And slowly she watched
5.2.	his eyes move slowly back
5.3.	the book trembling – briefly –
5.4.	in the heat.

The most striking sound pattern in this poem is the consonance of the velar stops /k/, /g/ (with the voiceless /k/ being more prominent): In verse 1: 'looked', 'book'; verse 2: 'look', 'looked' 'garden' 'japonica'; verse 3: 'spoke' 'again'; verse 4: 'can't', 'explain' (/ekspleɪn/), 'again', 'neck'; verse 5: 'back', 'book'. 'Book' and 'look', 'again' and 'explain' also rhyme. We note that these four words are all very important in the poem and some are repeated. 'Neck' at the end of verse 4 marks a climax or turning point in the

poem, reinforced by its consonance with 'back' in 5.2 and 'book' in
5.3. As the poem falls away in verse 5 from this climax at the end of
verse 4, we find the important word 'back' alliterating with 'book'
and 'briefly', both words that have also occurred in the first part of
the poem.

The final word 'heat' has assonance with 'briefly'. The final
consonant in 'heat' is a stop – but an alveolar stop /t/, not the
velar stop /k/ which we have heard throughout the poem. Another
/k/ here in the last word of the poem might be felt as excessive
and too 'pat' as a consonant rhyme with the climactic 'neck' at the
end of verse 4. A subtler effect is produced by this final /t/ having
near-consonance with its voiced pair /d/ in 'stirred' at the end of
verse 3. And this final /t/ has occurred twice earlier in combination
with /k/ at the end of the important word 'looked':/lʊkt/ and in
combination with /tʃ/ at the end of 'perched':/pɜːtʃt/ in 2.4 and
'watched':/wɒtʃt/ coming at the end of 5.1.

IV

Return

1.1.	After a long time in the desert
1.2.	what is it that brings back poetry
1.3.	like water to the Negev?
2.1.	I don't know. Not virtue
2.2.	or debauchery, or any special hardship
2.3.	or sudden love.
3.1.	I'd better, anyhow,
3.2.	make the most of it,
3.3.	and say the proper blessing
3.4.	for such occasions.

Verse 1 is a question, verse 2 is the non-answer and verse 3 the
conclusion. Consonant rhyme is used to shape the poem, firstly
of course to mark the pauses at the end of verse 1 and verse 2:
Negev/love.

The open syllables 'know' in 2.1 and 'anyhow' in 3.1 with their
parallel zero final consonants (and each word having an /n/ in it

somewhere) also structure the poem, by introducing the verse 2 'non-answer' and then verse 3, which in spite of this non-answer, *moves* ('anyhow') to a conclusion.

The repeat of the affricate /tʃ/, followed by that of the related fricative /ʃ/ gives energy to the list in verse 2 in the words: virtue, debauchery, special, hardship. (This is assuming that virtue is pronounced /vɜːtʃuː/, which I think is now more common than the conservative RP or 'actorish' /vɜːtjuː/). 'Debauchery' also rhymes with 'poetry' on their final two (unstressed) syllables. From 3.2 onwards, as the poem moves towards a conclusion (in spite of halting in verse 2) perhaps the sibilants /s/, /z/, /tʃ/, /ʃ/, /ʒ/ (in 'most':/məʊst/; 'say':/seɪ; 'blessing':/blesɪŋ/; 'such':/sʌtʃ/; 'occasions':/əkeɪʒənz/, give a sense of 'oiling the works' (for movement). The /tʃ/ sound in 'such' and the /ʒ/ sound in 'occasions' also echo the /tʃ/ and /ʃ/ of the list in verse 2. And 'occasions', the poem's last word, echoes 'make' in 3.2 and 'say' in 3.3 with assonance of the diphthong /eɪ/.

V

Rowan Tree[6]

1.1.	Three boulders of granite
1.2.	step over the stream
1.3.	where the steep path hairpins
1.4.	at the head of the combe.

2.1.	Islanded here, splendid
2.2.	in all its full-berried vermilion,
2.3.	filtering sun through eager green,
2.4.	glowed the rowan tree,
2.5.	magic and exigent
2.6.	as when for True Thomas
2.7.	it marked the choice of ways.

3.1.	I kept still, filled my eyes,
3.2.	listened to water
3.3.	and for red deer,
3.4.	waited to be told. What?

| 4.1. | When the bright ordeal burnt out |
| 4.2. | I munched cold bun and cheese. |

4.3.	Later in London another rowan
4.4.	shone among drab donkey brown
4.5.	of terraces and pavement slabs
4.6.	recently rinsed by rain.
4.7.	Clearer with second sight.

Here are a few of the sound patterns. Verse 1 gains energy from the /s/ + /t/ alliteration of 'step', 'stream' and 'steep', also of /h/ in 'hairpins', 'head'. We have the consonant rhyme of 'stream' at the end of 1.2 and 'combe' at the end of 1.4.

In 2.1 we have the internal rhyme 'islanded' with 'splendid', the latter has /e/ assonance with 'berried' in 2.2. We have the assonance of 'eager', 'green' in 2.3, 'tree' in 2.4, and consonant rhymes 'vermilion' in 2.2, 'sun', 'green' in 2.3 and 'rowan' in 2.4. 'Rowan' in turn has assonance with 'glowed'. 'Magic' and 'exigent' share the /dʒ/ sound in the middle. We have the near consonant rhyme of the voiced/voiceless pair /s/,/z/ in 'Thomas', 'choice', 'ways', 'eyes' and the later 'cheese'.

Verses 2, 3 and 4 all have a particular sound effect to mark their first line. In 2.1 we had the internal rhyme 'islanded', 'splendid'. In 3.1 we have internal assonance 'still', 'filled' and in 4.1 we have the alternating /b/ then zero-consonant alliteration of 'bright ordeal burnt out'.

In verse 3, which is a quatrain like verse 1, we have an off-stress near-rhyme of 'wáter' and 'deer' at the end of lines 2 and 3. The stressed syllable of 'wáter' also has alliteration-plus-consonant rhyme with 'wáited' in 4.4 and the last word in the verse 'whát'. 'What' has consonant rhyme with 'out' at the end of 4.1 and the last word in the poem, 'sight' (4.7) is also an off-stress consonant rhyme with the earlier 'granite' at the end of 1.1.

In verse 4 we have the consonant rhymes of London, rowan, shone, brown and rain, assonance of 'munched' 'bun', 'London', the internal near rhyme of 'drab' with 'slabs', alliteration of 'recently' 'rinsed', 'rain', and of the last two words in the poem, 'second sight'.

We have quoted the above three poems in full to show how in their various ways they not only use sounds for patterning and density but to 'point' the poem, connect important words, mark the poem's progress, give it shape. We have purposely concluded these examples with the poem 'Rowan Tree' because trees in all their variety of size and shape will be used in the next chapter as a metaphor for shape in contemporary poetry. In this next chapter we consider poetic form and shape in more detail.

NOTES

1. From 'Intelligence' by Steve Duffy in *Balloon* (London: Mattock Press, 1989).
2. For more detailed technical information on the sounds of English see *Longman Pronunciation Dictionary* by J. C. Wells (Harlow, Longman 1990), *An Introduction to the Pronunciation of English* by A. C. Gimson, 4th edition revised by Susan Ramsaran (London: Edward Arnold, 1989), J. D. O'Connor *Phonetics* (London: Penguin, 1973).
3. In *An Introduction to the Pronunciation of English*.
4. A translation by D. L. from the poet's typescript is in *Nicaraguan New Time* (London: Journeyman, 1988).
5. Example I is from Kathleen McPhilemy, 'Nawroz: the Kurdish New Year, 21st March 1985' in *Witness to Magic*; example II is from 'Camden Town Garden' in *Keeping Heart*; example III is Anne Beresford, 'The Question' in *The Sele of the Morning*; example IV is A. C. Jacobs, 'Return' in *The Proper Blessing*. 'The Question' and 'Return' are both quoted in part as examples in Chapter 1, and in full here in Chapter 2.
6. Example V is 'Rowan Tree' by D. L. published in *Acumen* 14 (1991). Complete poem. The poem is included in the collection *Second Sight* due out shortly from Katabasis.

3

The Poem's Shape

Poems are written in lines, which may have a certain rhythm or metre. If a natural meaning break comes at the end of the line we call it *end-stopped*:

> My love is like a red red rose,
> that's newly sprung in June.

If the line ends in the middle of a phrase and the meaning break comes in the succeeding line, we call this a run-on line or use the French word *enjambement*. In the example below[1] there is also a pause in the middle of the line at the full stop after 'bear'. This is called a *caesura* — a break.

> The zoo has entered the town. First
> the blue lipped-rhino, then
> the gross bear. I can already hear
> the cry of the wild cats.

I personally do not like the habit of ending lines on small function words such as 'the' or 'of' for no good reason. I can see no point in calling such lines 'breath units': they are not, unless you indulge in wilful panting. The style of delivery to match, with unnatural pauses on such little words – sometimes called the 'Black Mountain' style – can be very irritating.

SHAPE AND PATTERN

A poem is made up of a number of lines arranged in a certain *shape*. We noted in examples given at the end of the Chapter 2 that sound patterns can be used to *shape* or *point* a poem. The

55

contemporary poet tries to let each poem find its own peculiar shape. Rhythm, sound-patterning, the thought process, the ordering and juxtaposition of images, the syntax, the search for economy will all contribute to this. We return to the contemporary poet's options later in this chapter but first we look at some traditional ways of shaping a poem. It is enjoyable to be able to recognise these when reading. It is a good exercise to attempt some of these forms – if only to develop technical skills. And these traditional forms are what the contemporary poet is moving on *from* to develop new and living poetry.

Poems may consist of *verses* – that is, divisions in the poem which are marked in writing by leaving a line-space. Traditionally, some poems are divided into *stanzas*, that is, verses repeating the same pattern. There are many traditional stanza forms and whole-poem forms. These patterns usually consist of a regular metre and a *rhyme scheme*. As we saw in Chapter 2, rhymes can occur anywhere in the line but with strongest effect at the end of the line. This *end rhyme* is the position where the rhyme helps most to memorise the poem, acts as a *mnemonic*, and also the position of the rhyme in most traditional rhyme schemes. We shall not list all of these patterns (those interested may consult, for instance, F. Stillman's *Poet's Manual*).[2] We merely give some important examples.

SOME TRADITIONAL STANZA FORMS

Four-Line Stanza or Quatrain

Ballad Stanza
The ballad stanza consists of four lines (a quatrain) written in what is called *common measure*, that is four stresses in lines 1 and 3 and three stresses in lines 2 and 4. Lines 2 and 4 must rhyme. We write this rhyme scheme : a.b.c.b. Many ballads, popular verses and hymns are written in this pattern. We have already seen an example of it in Chapter 1, the 'Ballad of Sir Patrick Spens'. Here is a different stanza of the same ballad:

a	Long long may their ladies sit
b	with their fans into their hand,
c	or e'er they see Sir Patrick Spens
b	come sailing to the land.

Some ballads are written in quatrains with four stresses in every line – called *long measure* – and the same a.b.c.b. rhyme scheme, like the 'Ballad of True Thomas':

a	He has gotten a coat of the even cloth,
b	and a pair of shoes of velvet green,
c	and till seven years were gone and past
b	True Thomas on earth was never seen.

Some ballads are written in quatrains rhymed a.b.a.b. – called alternate rhymes – as in this example from one of Wordsworth's *Lucy Poems*:

a	No motion has she now, no force;
b	she neither hears nor sees;
a	rolled round in earth's diurnal course
b	with rocks and stones and trees.

Rubai

The rubai (plural rubaiyat) is an iambic pentameter quatrain rhymed a.a.b.a. Edward Fitzgerald used it for his translation of Omar Khayyam. The contemporary Iranian-born poet Mimi Khalvati uses this form in a poem dedicated to her Persian grandmother:[3]

> '*Salaam, my daughter-lovely-as-the-moon!*'
> Would that the world could see me, Telajune,
> through your eyes! Or that I could see a world
> that takes such care to tend what fades so soon.

Three-Line Stanza or Tercet

Terza Rima

Terza Rima has a pattern of three-line stanzas rhymed a.b.a., b.c.b., c.d.c. and so on. This is the form in which Dante wrote his *Divine Comedy*. Dorothy Sayers used the form for her English translation, which is sometimes ingenious but seldom great poetry like the original :

a	As we read on, our eyes met now and then,
b	and to our cheeks the changing colour started,
a	but just one moment overcame us – when

b   we read of the smile, desired of lips long-thwarted.
c   such smile, by such a lover kissed away,
b   he that may never more from me be parted.

The *enjambement* of 'when' with the succeeding stanza produces an unintentionally comic effect comparable to Lewis Carroll's: 'When I found the door was shut/ I tried to turn the handle but...'

Two-Line Stanza or Couplet

A couplet is either a two-line stanza (which may rhyme or not) or two lines next to each other that rhyme but are not laid out as a separate stanza. The heroic couplet is iambic pentameter rhyming a.a. Pope was famous for his.

a   Know then thyself, presume not God to scan;
a   the proper study of mankind is man.

It is extremely difficult for a contemporary poet to write a rhyming couplet that does not thump or sound trite, so caution is required. However it can be a useful form – for instance, for satirical attacks on political enemies.

PATTERNS USING REPETITION OF WORDS OR IDEAS

Refrain

Phrases or lines repeated in the course of a poem, sometimes with slight variation are, called a *refrain*. Perhaps one of the most famous examples in modern poetry is the Spanish poet García Lorca's Lament for his friend, the bullfighter Ignacio Sánchez Mejías. The first section of the poem has the refrain: 'At five in the afternoon.' In Section 2, 'The Spilt Blood', the refrain is: 'I don't want to see it' ('¡Que no quiero verla!') repeated as 'I do not want to see the blood.'
    Refrains often come in ballads as in the question repeated at the beginning of every stanza:

Where have you been, Lord Randal my son?

When a whole stanza is repeated regularly this is called a *chorus*.

Parallelism and Antiphony

The psalms are the most famous example of parallelism. Each verse expresses the same thought twice in parallel form. This pattern is called *antiphonal*, because the second part of the verse *responds* to the first. Here is part of Psalm 114:

> The sea saw and fled
> > Jordan turned back.
> The mountains skipped like rams
> > and the hills like little lambs.
> Sea, what was the matter, that you fled?
> > Jordan, why did you turn back?
> Mountains, what made you skip like rams
> > and you hills like little lambs?
> At the presence of the Lord the earth shook,
> > at the presence of the God of Jacob.

A modern example is a poem by the Chilean poet Maria Eugenia Bravo Calderara, simply called 'Psalm':[4]

> And towards Adam her footsteps went,
> towards him she would always make her way,
> because love is movement against time,
> love is a flooding river against death
> and unlove is a dry and dusty watercourse, unlife.

TRADITIONAL POEM FORMS

There are also many traditional forms for whole poems. We do not list all of them here (again consult Frances Stillman's *Poet's Manual* if you want to look them up). Here we choose as examples two traditional forms which contemporary poets have found well worth attempting.

Villanelle

This elaborate form has two refrains, whose repetitions give the form a certain hypnotic quality. The form developed from a round song (compare the song 'Now Welcome Summer' sung by the birds at the end of Chaucer's *Parliament of Fowls*). It has an odd number of three-line stanzas rhymed a.b.a. followed by a quatrain rhymed a.b.a.a. The first and third lines of the first stanza (both 'a' rhymes) are repreated in alternate stanzas as the alternating refrain. Here is a modern example, Dylan Thomas's 'Do Not Go Gentle into that Good Night'.[5] All the lines of the poem rhyme with either 'night' or 'day'. The refrain marked A1 or the refrain marked A2 is repeated at the end of each succeeding stanza alternately and both are repeated at the end of the poem:

A1	Do not go gentle into that good night,
b	old age should burn and rave at close of day;
A2	rage, rage, against the dying of the light.
a	Though wise men at their end know dark is right,
b	because their words had forked no lightning they
A1	do not go gentle into that good night.
a	Good men, the last wave by, crying how bright
b	their frail deeds might have danced in a green bay,
A2	rage, rage against the dying of the light.
a	Wild men, who caught and sang the sun in flight,
b	and learn, too late, they grieved it on its way,
A1	do not go gentle into that good night.
a	Grave men, near death, who see with blinding sight
b	blind eyes could blaze like meteors and be gay,
A2	rage, rage against the dying of the light.
a	And you, my father, there on the sad height,
b	curse, bless, me now with your fierce tears, I pray.
A1	Do not go gentle into that good night.
A2	Rage, rage against the dying of the light.

Sonnet

The most famous early sonnet writer was the Italian poet Petrarch. The Italian sonnet has fourteen lines divided into an *octet* (the first eight lines) and a *sestet* (the last six lines). The sestet develops the thought or idea (also called 'conceit' from the Italian 'concetto': 'concept') expounded in the octet. The rhyme scheme is a.b.b.a., a.b.b.a., c.d.e., c.d.e. So it needs four 'a' rhymes and four 'b' rhymes – quite a lot for English. Milton wrote sonnets in the Italian form. The sonnet 'On His Blindness', breaks for 'part 2' (the sestet) in the middle of the eighth line (marked #), rather than at the end of it.

> When I consider how my light is spent
> ere half my days, in this dark world and wide,
> and that one talent, which is death to hide
> lodged with me useless, though my soul more bent
> to serve therewith my Maker and present
> my true account, lest he returning chide.
> 'Doth God exact day-labour, light denied?'
> I fondly ask. # But patience to prevent
> that murmur, soon replies, 'God doth not need
> either man's work or his own gifts, who best
> bear his mild yoke, they serve him best, his state
> is kingly: thousands at his bidding speed
> and post o'er land and ocean without rest.
> They also serve who only stand and wait.'

The English or Shakespearean sonnet is written in iambic pentameter and divided into three quatrains plus a rhyming couplet. Often each quatrain develops the sonnet's thought or 'conceit' and the final couplet provides a conclusion. The rhyme scheme is as follows: a.b.a.b./ c.d.c.d./ e.f.e.f./ g.g. In the following example by Shakespeare the thought does develop from quatrain to quatrain. But there is also a more marked development after the first eight lines as the poet moves on to say why 'thy eternal summer shall not fade' (because of this sonnet!). So we find this sonnet divides into three quatrains plus couplet and also into an octet and a sestet:

> Shall I compare thee to a summer's day?
> Thou art more lovely and more temperate.
> Rough winds do shake the darling buds of May,
> and summer's lease hath all too short a date.
> Sometime too hot the eye of heaven shines,
> and often is his gold complexion dimmed;
> and every fair from fair some time declines,

by chance, or nature's changing course, untrimmed.#
But thy eternal summer shall not fade,
nor lose possession of that fair thou ow'st,
nor shall Death brag thou wand'rest in his shade,
when in eternal lines to time thou grow'st.
So long as men can breathe or eyes can see,
so long lives this, and this gives life to thee.

Perhaps the chief difficulty with the Shakespearean sonnet is to produce a satisfactory final couplet. Contemporary poets use various devices to deal with it, such as turning it into a question, to make the poem more 'open-ended'. It is a good exercise to write sonnets but another curious problem arises. It is very habit-forming and once you begin it is hard to stop! This may explain why the sixteenth century sonneteers tended to write such lengthy sonnet sequences. It can become an addiction.

VERSE PARAGRAPH

Milton divided his long poems such as *Paradise Lost* into *paragraphs* of unequal length. Contemporary poets often write poems with verses or sections of unequal length dictated by the sense or syntax. Ernesto Cardenal's *Cosmic Canticle*,[6] which is comparable in length to *Paradise Lost*, is written in verse paragraphs. The poem is divided into *cantigas*, which are complete poems in themselves. When I first read the *cantiga* 'The Music of the Spheres', it appeared to sprawl. But after reading it a few times and letting it sink in, I became aware how the verse paragraphs are linked and closely interwoven with a dense pattern of recurring images and themes. Slowly I began to grasp the poem's shape and hear it as one piece of music. I think I was helped by the majestic and idiosyncratic shapes of the great London plane trees waving outside my second-floor window.

FORM IN CONTEMPORARY POETRY

T. S Eliot writes:[7]

Only a bad poet could welcome free verse as a liberation from form. It was a revolt against dead form, and a preparation for new form or for the renewal of the old; it was an insistence upon the inner unity which is unique to every poem, against the outer unity which is typical.

The contemporary poet tries to let each poem find its own individual shape. What makes us or a poem individual is the *body* – in the poem's case, the body of words. Every good poem must come to life as an organic body – an organic body doing something, dancing perhaps. In Chapter 1 the poem's rhythm was compared to the heartbeat. The ordering and juxtaposition of images, sound-patterning, the thought process or sequence of ideas, the syntax are like the body's other parts and processes. These should all work together with nothing wasted to create the poem's economy. Padding or verbosity may produce fatty degeneration of the heart or cancer.

As now each poem must find its own individual shape, the possibilities are endless. Contemporary poets often prefer an irregular shape because a closed pattern would be too neat or 'pat' for their purpose. Adapting Yeats, we may think of much contemporary poetry as a rough shape, its hour come round at last, struggling to be born alive. Or we could develop our comparison of contemporary poems with trees. Most contemporary poets do not attempt such huge poems as *Paradise Lost*, Derek Walcott's *Omeros* or Cardenal's *Cosmic Canticle*. Each poem must find its own form, and each humble hawthorn has as individual a shape as each giant oak or beech. Trees come in all sizes, but large or small, the thing that often impresses us most about a tree is how very *present* it is in its shape. The shape is what makes it both very much there, self-contained, and present to our eyes. The same is true of hills, which sometimes seem to crouch like huge beasts with 'flanks'. If you look straight into the sun on a bright day and then turn with your back to the sun and look at a tree or a hill (or both) you see the shape more distinctly, sometimes even 'numinously'.

Hopkins calls this 'inscape'. A poem with a good shape, however irregular, will have a similar presence to our ears. When the poem is 'right' it will have beauty: 'the shining of shape' (*splendor formae*) and peace: 'the tranquillity of order' (*tranquillitas ordinis*). It needs practice to hear a shape, let alone produce one. It is essential to listen and read widely to discover which poems have this kind of *presence*, as a living sound-shape. Likewise when you have written a poem, test it on other people's ears.

The rhythms and sounds of English are yours. All contemporary poetry and also the traditional metres and forms are at your disposal, but not for mechanical imitation or pastiche. A poem made today must sound original, not stale or archaic. (It is probably better for a new poet to be very sparing with rhymes.) English speakers have a common stock – like a gene pool, perhaps – from which to select and combine to create each new individual poem. We inherit all this wealth to spend freely. It is fatal to imagine that being the heir means you have a position to keep up and must behave according to a protocol. This wealth is a wealth to delight a socialist rather than a conservative or hack marketeer. Possession does not mean others are dispossessed. However rich you are and the more you spend, you are not depriving anyone else but adding to the common wealth of all.

Contemporary poetry takes innumerable shapes. Three qualities above all are required: *economy*: much in little; *beauty*: the shine *on* the shape or *from within* the shape (Hopkins' distinction between 'inscape' and 'instress') and thirdly, *peace*: the tranquillity of order, the sense that the order of the words, lines and verses of a poem have to be this way and no other. The shaping may be highly subtle and complex or more obvious. Success depends on whether the purpose is satisfied.

At the end of the last chapter we looked at how the poems 'Return', The Question' and 'Rowan Tree' used sound patterning to provide shape. Look at these poems again in the light of what has been said in this chapter and note the other shaping factors besides sound patterning. For example, 'Rowan Tree' has four verses with 4 and 7 lines alternately. Each of these poems has its own shape, idiosyncratic as that of the rowan tree itself. Now we add two more examples, each with a trimmer, more 'cultivated' shape taking what it wants from traditional forms but not strictly *conforming* either.

EXAMPLES

I

The first example is a poem of three eight line stanzas, each consisting of two quatrains rhyming or chiming (sometimes with near rhymes, consonant rhymes, off-stress rhymes) a.b.c.b. Most of the lines are in three-stress sprung rhythm, with occasional lines having only two stresses and a couple of lines having four. One of the first things we notice is the *refrain*: 'Buzz!' said the blue-fly in his head.' (The poet tells us in a footnote that Titus was afflicted with a fly buzzing in his head after he had destroyed the Temple in Jerusalem.)

Titus and Berenice [8]

'Turn to me in the darkness,
    Asia with your cool
gardens beyond the desert,
    your clear, frog-haunted pool;
I seek your reassurance –
    forget, as I would forget,
your holy city cast down, the Temple
    that still I desecrate.'

'Buzz!' said the blue-fly in his head.

'In darkness master me,
    Rome with your seven hills,
roads, rhetorical aqueducts,
    and ravaging eagles;
worlds are at bitter odds, yet we
    can find our love at least –
not expedient to the Senate,
    abominable to the priest.'

'Buzz!' said the blue-fly in his head.

Titus the clement Emperor
    and she of Herod's house
slobbered and clawed each other
    like creatures of the stews;
lay together, then lay apart
    and knew they had not subdued –
she the insect in his brain,
    nor he her angry God.

We note that the first two stanzas, as well as having the same form, are also *antiphonal* because in the first Titus speaks and in the second Berenice responds, each saying what attracts him or her to the other. The parallelism lies in the almost archetypical *contrast* between the male and the female. The third verse succinctly tells their story. We have another contrasting parallel: both were high born but both behaved 'like creatures of the stews' together. After they 'lay apart' their fate still remained in some way parallel in what they had 'not subdued'. The poem's shape expresses with classical economy the relation of its two subjects both when they 'lay together' and when they 'lay apart'.

II

The second example looks again at example number six at the end of the Chapter 1. Here we look at its shape.

Song

> Mistakes heartache
> unexpected defeat
> burnt all black
> dead beat.
>
> Fire charred the heath
> death dried the heart.
> They who hated this earth
> have deeply scarred.
>
> Yet deeper the seed
> love sheds its life.
> Blood stopped stone dead.
> Moist warmth unfurls leaf.
>
> My hope is red petal
> heart beat.

This poem has three quatrains with rhymes or consonant rhyme a.b.a.b. and a final unrhyming couplet. Therefore it has fourteen lines divided up as in a Shakespearean sonnet, but it is not in iambic pentameter (its rhythm has been analysed at the end of Chapter 1) and does not have a final rhyming couplet. This shape is emphasised by the syntactic patterning of past simple verbs in verses 1 and 2, and present simple verbs (except the past recap 'stopped') in verses 3 and 4. Internal sound patterning also points the shape. In the first verse as well as the consonant rhyme of ache/black and the strong rhyme defeat/beat, we have the assonance of takes/ache, which also have the consonance of /k/, continued in 'unexpected' and 'black'. In the last two lines of this verse we have the alliteration of 'burnt', ' black', 'beat', all stressed monosyllables. In verse 2 the first line ending 'heath' has assonance with the last word of the previous verse 'beat'; 'heath' also alliterates with the last word in 2.2 'heart', it has consonant rhyme with 'death' at the beginning of 2.2 as well as its consonant rhyme (in accordance with the rhyme scheme) with 'earth' at the end of 2.3 'Charred' in 2.1 has consonant rhyme as well as syntactic similarity with 'dried' in 2.2, it has assonance with 'heart' at the end of 2.2 and rhymes with 'scarred' at the end of 2.4. 'Scarred' in its turn (in accordance with the rhyme scheme) nearly rhymes with 'heart' in 2.2, that is, they have the same vowels and their final consonants are the voiced/voiceless pair /t/, /d/. In the final couplet the poem's last line 'heart beat' echoes and contrasts with the fourth line of verse 1: 'dead beat'. The 'upbeat' contrast with the two previous mentions of heart: 'heartache' and 'death dried the heart' is reinforced by the contrasting 'black' in verse 1 and 'red' in the last verse. The poem attempts to work on several levels, one of which is personal. On a more public level, it was written not long after the Sandinista election defeat in 1990 and black and red are the Sandinista colours.

NOTES

1. From Elaine Feinstein, 'The First Siren', in *The Celebrants* (London: Hutchinson, 1973).

2. Frances Stillman, *Poet's Manual and Rhyming Dictionary* (London: Thames and Hudson, 1966).

3. Mimi Khalvati, 'Rubaiyat' in *Persian Miniatures* (Huddersfield: Smith-Doorstop, 1989).

4. 'Psalm' by María Eugenia Bravo Calderara in *Prayer in the National Stadium* (London: Katabasis, 1992).

5. Dylan Thomas, *The Poems 1934–53* (London: Everyman Classic edition, J. M. Dent and Sons, 1982).

6. *Cántico Cósmico* by Ernesto Cardenal (Managua: Editorial Nueva Nicaragua, 1989). *The Music of the Spheres* is a translation of one *cantiga* of the *Cosmic Canticle* by D. L. (London: Katabasis, 1990).

7. From 'The Music of Poetry' in *On Poetry and Poets*.

8. Example I is 'Titus and Berenice' by John Heath-Stubbs in *Collected Poems* (Manchester: Carcanet, 1988).

4
Content

Poets used to be called seers and the germ of a poem is a moment of intense seeing (which includes feeling), an *insight*, becoming a 'seeing how to say it', which both clarifies the seeing for the seer ('how can I know what I mean till I hear what I say?') and *deprivatises* it through language, so that others see with you. In George Herbert's words, it is 'something understood'. The seeing may be the literal seeing of something before our eyes, combining with feelings, thoughts and experiences – possibly right back to 'pre-verbal experience' – in a new awareness ('now I see'), whose energy seeks an outlet in creation which, as *language*, is also able to overcome intolerable isolation. When language has a lot of psychic energy and is very concentrated, it becomes poetry. The preceding three chapters on rhythm, sound and form describe some of the ways in which a poem may accumulate energy and concentration. In a poem economy is not meanness or sensual thrift but fitness, so that it can do a lot in a little, nothing is wasted and a minimum produces the maximum wealth of meaning and power. The material of poetry is the spoken word, which is performed and must also actively *perform*. Technically, we say the language of poetry is not merely *referential* – that is, talking about something – it is *performative*, it does something. It does something for the poet, in that only when the poem is finished is this particular seeing done and it does something for the listener or to the listener (it 'does something to me', 'it gives me a buzz'); the poem's energy and intensity of meaning are communicated: it *works*. The power of some poems operates not only on the first occasion we hear them – performed or with inward ear – but stays with us, perhaps permanently.

In Chapter 1 we noted how we may feel and see differently at different times according to our body's rhythms. Our bodily state is one of several factors determining our mood, our receptiveness to the world around us and our ability to produce or appreciate poetry. A famous example is of course Coleridge's 'Dejection: An Ode':

> All this long eve, so balmy and serene,
> have I been gazing at the western sky,
> and its peculiar tint of yellow green.
> And still I gaze – and with how blank an eye!
> And those thin clouds above, in flakes and bars,
> that give away their motion to the stars . . .
>
> I see them all so excellently fair,
> *I see, not feel, how beautiful they are.*

The really terrible thing about this dejection, he says, is not that it takes away any feeling of cheerfulness, but that it paralyses his gift for poetry:

> But oh! each visitation
> suspends what nature gave me at my birth,
> my shaping spirit of imagination.

Anyone who has suffered from depression will sympathise with Coleridge in this torment. (However, we cannot fail to note the paradox that 'Dejection: An Ode' is one of the finest poems he ever produced.)

ECONOMY AND INTENSITY

A poem's energy gives it its intensity. This energy is likely to be greater if the poet taps and articulates deep, perhaps even unconscious or pre-verbal forces within. Economy means that this intensity is *concentrated* in the poem and no word is wasted. This means that *simplicity* is to be preferred to wilful obscurity; it is uneconomic for a poem to be more difficult than it need be to say what it wants. It means that *freshness* is to be preferred to staleness because stale expressions have lost their impact and are therefore uneconomic.

As the principle of economy means a lot in a little, the poem and the poet's work as a whole will be greater, the wider the scope of its vision and spirit. A poem may be well crafted but slight if 'the matter is trivial'. This does not mean that the subject matter of every poem must be 'cosmic' but that a poem will have more value if it belongs to a (perhaps developing) wholeness and generosity and the poet, over time, is building up a coherent and consistent *body of work*.

PARTICULARITY: IMAGES

The language of poetry communicates primarily to our senses. We hear the poem spoken and these sounds are also words whose meaning can strike all our senses, often beginning with our sense of sight. A poem conveys its meaning in *images* and obviously, we are better able to see what it is saying when the images are clear and *particular*. So unlike the opening of a love poem by a now famous critic: 'Some people, like some flowers, disclose themselves to the trained eye only,' it is better to particularise, like Perdita offering her Florizel 'daffodils that come before the swallow dares . . . violets . . . pale primroses. . .'

Words can appeal to our sense of hearing not only by their actual sound but also by their meaning and again, more so, if they are particular rather than general or abstract. A scene is conjured more graphically if we not only see how it looks but hear how it sounds. We have many words which appeal to our senses of sight and hearing, a medium number for touch and fewer for smell and taste. It is hard to describe a smell or taste the reader has not experienced, for example coffee, a sponge cake baked on a tansy leaf, Turkish delight. But smell and taste once summoned have the power to recall a particular moment in the past more strongly than any of the other senses. Proust's famous biscuit vividly recalled childhood and García Lorca reminds us how powerfully a special smell and the taste of a local sweet brings back a particular place. In his *Spiritual Exercises*, which had such a strong effect on Hopkins among many others, Ignatius of Loyola suggests that a meditation should begin with a 'composition of place': to imagine in detail where the scene or event we are contemplating occurs. Then he recommends an application of the five senses: 'see the people with the eye of the imagination . . . listen with your hearing to what they are saying . . . smell with your nose . . . taste with your tastebuds . . . feel with your touch . . .'

Particular people, perhaps even named, also usually have more impact in a poem than a general reference to a sociological group: 'Peter the roofer fell into debt and lost his house in Kentish Town where he was born' is better than 'A high proportion of C1 and C2 first time buyers could not sustain mortgage repayments when the interest rates increased, and were repossessed'. We also note that although the former sentence beginning with Peter is shorter and simpler, it conveys more concrete information. Some of the most memorable first world war poems are those involving individuals. Siegfried Sassoon's 'The Dug-Out':

> Why do you lie with your legs ungainly huddled,
> and one arm bent across your sullen, cold,
> exhausted face? It hurts my heart to watch you . . .

Wilfrid Owen's 'Futility':

> Move him into the sun –
> gently its touch awoke him once,
> at home, whispering of fields unsown.

Or the climactic line of 'Strange Meeting' (we clearly hear the tone of voice):

> I am the enemy you killed, my friend.

Particular images strike us literally but may also act as symbols or comparisons. Then the language becomes *figurative*. (See below under *figurative language* for *metaphors*, *similes* and other *figures of speech*). In poetry the particular is often what has the most universal resonance and particular images may be used to convey, illustrate or develop *ideas*.

IDEAS AND FEELINGS

Poetry operates firstly through images which are perceived by our senses, but it also conveys ideas. An idea may be a 'conceit' upon which a sonnet turns or it may be something understood, a thought or principle arising out of or illustrated by the image or series of images. Ideas may be purely intellectual but have more force in poetry when they are associated with *feelings*. The poem 'Futility' quoted above is a model example. Here is the full text:

> Move him into the sun –
> gently its touch awoke him once,
> at home, whispering of fields unsown.
> Always it woke him, even in France,
> until this morning and this snow.
> If anything might rouse him now
> the kind old sun will know.
>
> Think how it wakes the seeds, –
> woke, once, the clays of a cold star.
> Are limbs, so dear-achieved, are sides,
> full-nerved – still warm – too hard to stir?
> Was it for this the clay grew tall?
> O what made fatuous sunbeams toil
> to break earth's sleep at all?

As we saw, the first line focuses on a particular individual and the actual words of this line could well be exactly what someone said: 'Move him into the sun'. We hear these words said on a particular occasion, which is also presented to our eyes. We gather he is from the country (an earlier draft had 'in Wales' in place of 'at home'), perhaps a ploughboy whom the sun awoke 'whispering of fields unsown'. In the second and final verse, whose form repeats that of the first, the *idea* is developed via the ploughed fields already evoked: 'Think how it wakes the seeds'. The image of ploughland is continued to conjure up the whole process of evolution: 'woke once the clays of a cold star', whose age-long labours have finally delivered humanity: 'limbs, so dear-achieved'. How futile all this labour seems with the sun powerless to stir this boy lying dead as a stillborn child.

> O what made fatuous sunbeams toil
> to break earth's sleep at all?

The poem develops an idea, which also articulates a feeling. It is the combination of heard spoken words, visual image, idea and strong feeling – so much within the formal constraint of two identically patterned seven line verses – that gives this poem it is extraordinary power.

Ernesto Cardenal's poem 'Meditation in a DC-10'[1] begins:

> I don't know why I remembered Novalis' phrase:
> 'Touching a naked body is touching heaven.'
> The military pilot opened his map of our country
> to show the dark little girl of nine
> (it was our land below)
> and his hand brushed her small hand . . .

The poet meditating in the aeroplane sees the vivid image of the pilot's hand brushing the little girl's. He goes on to consider a whole range of particular human touching leading up to his *idea* of communism in the last line:

> Breastfeeding a baby,
> a couple deeply caressing,
> holding hands,
> clasping a shoulder,
> human touching human
> human skin meeting human skin
> is putting your finger on communism *compañeros*.

The images illustrate the poet's idea and also his feeling about what communism – 'heaven on earth' – should be. The introduction of the abstract word 'communism' in the last line acts as a startling polemic to those who would disagree, whereas for those who would agree with him it is a shock resolution of the tension that has been building up in the list just before it – a shock of recognition.

An idea may be a question rather than a solution, as for example in this poem by Kathleen McPhilemy 'Is Love the Word?':[2]

> I fell in love with the man who was poetry;
> his head shone like a torch, above the ordinary . . .
>
> . . . still when I see, too far behind me
> or in front, a certain way of hair,

the crowds and pavements fade, as I am lost
in a return of cloudy brightness.

Thus the real word is made difficult:
though I cleave to you, forsaking all other . . .
the spirit loves, but body cringes or swells
with small angers, daily awkwardness and all
the complications of living we are tangled in.
Is love the word? Is love the same word?

The poem begins with an image of 'the man who was poetry' with
'a certain way of hair', moves on through the 'daily awkwardness'
of living together to reflect on the meaning of love. Part of the
reason for the puzzled questions in the last line is that these two
experiences *feel* very different.

Poetry seeks to 'see'. Sometimes we do not see how something
was until it is over. Mayakovsky recommends a change of place
in order to look back over something with a clear perspective. This
is one of the functions of the pastoral in the English tradition. A
spell in the country is often not just a holiday or an idyll but an
enlightening retreat, as the Forest of Arden is for the protagonists
in *As You Like It*.

We may not agree with the ideas expressed in a poem or
sympathise with the feelings. We may still admire some of the
poem's qualities, its technical skill, its vivid images, the way in
which the ideas develop from the images, its cleverness, its ambition
and so on. We may even enjoy a poem very much while profoundly
disagreeing with the poet's ideas. Some Italian communists admire
the fascist poet D'Annunzio. There are feminists who consider
Donne sexist but find his love poetry delicious, an atheist may be
deeply moved by Hopkins' 'Wreck of the Deutschland'. It is not a
bad thing to be able to admire good poetry written by poets with
whom we disagree and it is useful to try and work out what exactly
it is we do admire in the poem. Perhaps the poem may even broaden
our sympathies or we may end up saying, this poem is well written
but I disagree with it. But there is a unique delight in *recognising*
our own inmost feelings and convictions expressed in an excellent
poem.

We may also enjoy poetry that is witty and trivial, comic verse,
light verse, doggerel for an occasion and so on. For example some of
Wendy Cope's parodies are hilarious, particularly her Wordsworth

'Baa Baa Black Sheep'.[3] We do not always feel like being deep and noble. But we should enjoy light verse for what it is. We cannot survive on a diet of lemon meringue pie, however fond of it we are. This leads on to the question of poetry's *scope*.

SCOPE

One limitation on the scope of poetry may be the consideration that other art forms can do something better. It is unusual to find very long narrative poems being written in England today, possibly because some of the functions these used to fulfil have now been taken over by film. But as poetry is language at its most intensely alive no human culture can do without it.

Each poem is a fresh look at the visible world and may also contain a fresh *insight*. Poem by poem these insights may add up to a *view* of the world. Gradually the poet may produce a *body of work* striving for coherence. There should be no arbitrary limitations placed on the scope of this work. Of course not every poem will address the whole cosmos. As we saw, poems are primarily concerned with particularities: the back of a lover's neck, feeling like shaking your screaming child, swimming with friends in Highgate Ladies' Pond, discovering an enemy, goings-on in the street, things in the house, a patterned carpet, a pile of rubbish, a garden with old brickwork, all kinds of flowers, bees, moles . . .

But as poetry is concerned with *seeing*, one criterion for great poetry must be the *scope* of the poet's vision. Inwards and outwards. Self-awareness grows by articulation and poem by poem a good poet will release into the light of language increasing depths of his or her inner, perhaps unconscious self, violent loves and hates, mutilations and so on. This does not necessarily have to be in confessional verse. The energies of this chaos may be poured into images in the external world, impersonal ideas, sympathetic identification with other people. But it is this psychic energy that gives poetry its force. Unless our spirit broods over this chaos *within ourselves* and finds shapes for it to express itself in, we create nothing.

The starting point of our poetry must be ourselves. The experience of any human being is equally valid as a starting point for poetry. A culture which privileged the experience of an 'elite' and excluded or undervalued poetry expressing the experience of 'outsiders': women, children, black or working class people would be greatly impoverished. More will be said about this in Chapter 5. But poetry's scope should not be confined to ourselves. The admirable feminist axiom 'the personal is the political' should not mean that my concern in world politics is reduced to my moods and domestic quarrels. Everything connects and poetry is greater if it makes these connections. The logical goal of economy and concentration – a lot in a little – is to embrace as much as possible within the finite space of our poetry, not just 'my personal life', but 'myself in the world', 'the world in which I am', 'the cosmos in which we are'. This cannot exclude politics.

The present poetry 'establishment' in Britain are often wary of political poetry that challenges the status quo *at home* and may try to dismiss it as 'mere propaganda', *ipso facto* bad poetry. Assuming the rightness or superiority of British and US capitalism is called 'keeping politics out of poetry'.

Of course the quality of political poems must be judged in the same way as other poems for their economy, intensity, particularity, freshness and poetic skill in general. Right-on doggerel is not poetry. But it is a severe limitation to confine the subject matter of poetry to what is considered 'good manners' or 'good form' or 'good taste' by a smug bourgeoisie. This is in direct opposition to poetry which embodies a wholeness of vision and generosity of spirit to the limit of human potential – greater than any gods humanity have imagined to date. In 'The Fall of Hyperion', Keats' unfinished testament on his poetic pilgrimage, he says:

> whereon there grew
> a power within me of enormous ken
> to see as a god sees, and take the depth
> of things as nimbly as the outward eye
> can size and shape pervade . . .

In the Genesis story Adam and Eve were forbidden to eat the apple because 'when you eat it your eyes will be opened, and you will be like God, knowing good and evil'.

We should judge the quality of poetry not only by its technical skill but by the truth and scope of its *seeing*. The poet should try to see things as they are, including a salutary self-knowledge and a willingness to look at the real world. The language of politicians and war reporters is sometimes designed to deceive or at least to lull the imagination: 'carpet bombing' (what is the carpet made of?), 'surgical strike' (who is healed?), 'taken out' meaning killed. Or, in the 'Allies' advance on Kuwait, the term 'taken out' was used to mean its direct opposite: ploughed in and buried alive. After his seven year apprenticeship True Thomas, the Rhymer, received a gift that he could never lie. He became a 'soothsayer' (truth-teller): a poet. The poet's role as seer *must* be subversive, not only to point out and challenge what is dehumanising in the actual state of the world but to assume full humanity by challenging God and eating the 'forbidden fruit', to imagine a heaven on *earth*. In order to be subversive poetry does not need to be polemical, merely to refuse to accept arbitrary limitations on its scope.

Something of what is meant by becoming 'like God' is described in the theology of the trinity – an astonishing description of the potential of the human spirit. In this schema the first person is Being, which expresses itself in Word. As this Word is a totally adequate expression, it too is personal, the second person, who not only is 'with God' but 'is God'. And just as naturally as being flows into word, word flows into Love, the third person. (When we are happy with a poem we have produced and even more when we hear great poetry performed, part of what we feel is love.) In this theology the world is made by the divine Word. Creation is *poesis*: making. It is true that we shape and create our world by language and poetry is language in power. But we make poetry, we make the Word.

García Lorca calls the power of poetry the *duende*,[4] 'a mysterious power that everyone feels but that no philosopher has explained':

> The *duende* is a power and not a behaviour, it is a struggle and not a concept . . . with the *duende* it is easier to love and to understand . . . It gives the sensation of freshness wholly unknown, having the quality of a newly created rose, of miracle, and produces in the end an almost religious enthusiasm. In Arabic . . . the appearance of the *duende* is greeted with vociferous shouts of 'Alá! Alá!': 'God! God!'

ALLUSION

Poets write within a language tradition and we say more about this in the Chapter 5. One way in which poems are enriched and made denser is by allusions or echoes. This has to be done with care: an over-used quotation will have the effect of cliché and if the allusion is too obscure for the reader it will mystify rather than communicate.

In her 'Thoughts about the Person from Porlock'[5] Stevie Smith reflects on the well known story of Coleridge being interrupted in the writing of 'Kubla Khan' by a person from Porlock:

> Coleridge received the Person from Porlock
> and ever after called him a curse,
> then why did he hurry to let him in?
> He could have hid in the house . . . .
>
> I long for the Person from Porlock
> to bring my thoughts to an end,
> I am becoming impatient to see him
> I think of him as a friend.

This poem is more enjoyable for the reader who knows the Porlock story and is familiar with 'Kubla Khan'. (Although 'Kubla Khan' stops in a the middle of the story, is the poem really unfinished, where could it go from there, is the poet talking about himself, and so on?) But the poem is also a fine example of Stevie Smith's work with its subtle interweaving tones: teasing, gently debunking, comic, with her wry self-knowledge we apply to ourselves (very ready to be interrupted when writing is difficult), and her longing for death.

In another poem, 'The Word', Stevie Smith begins with an echo of Wordsworth's 'Rainbow':

> My heart leaps up with streams of joy,

This is the starting point for her poem which in fact points out her *difference* from Wordsworth. She continues:

> my lips tell of drouth;
> why should my heart be full of joy
> and not my mouth?
>
> I fear the Word, to speak or write it down,
> I fear all that is brought to birth and born;
> this fear has turned my joy into a frown.

We have no trouble understanding this poem if we do not get the Wordsworth echo, but the echo enriches it.

In his poem 'Turnham Green'[6] the learned John Heath-Stubbs relates:

> I met one face I seemed to know –
> the ghost of Ugo Foscolo;
> he said: 'The year that Byron shook
> the dust of England off I took
> the devious paths the exile knows . . .
>
> To Soho first then Camden Town.
> At St John's Wood I lived and sang
> with oranges and lemons to hang
> on boughs of English trees in vain –
> Zante would not come again.

We enjoy this poem more if we know Foscolo's work ('Nè più mai toccherò le sacre sponde . . . Zacinto mia . . . ': 'Never again will I tread your holy shores . . . my Zante' and his complaint that fate has prescribed him 'illacrimata sepoltura': an 'unwept burial'.) And also if we know that he was buried at Turnham Green. Perhaps many English readers will not have this knowledge about the Italian poet. But Stubbs' poem tells us enough to realise that Foscolo is an Italian poet contemporary of Byron's, exiled to London and feeling alien in a land where oranges and lemons do not grow on the trees. It is still a pleasure to imagine (the blind) John Heath-Stubbs' encounter with the ghost of Foscolo in Turnham Green and for a Londoner there is also the (not to be despised) simple pleasure of hearing London names on the lips of the Italian poet. (I live in Camden Town!)

A poem on 'The Death of Allende'[7] written shortly after the event was dismissed by a critic as 'reminiscent of E. J. Thribb' because he was not only unsympathetic to the subject but apparently did not *hear* any of the allusions which add density to the plain language. For example, there is an echo of Lorca's Lament for his friend Ignacio Sanchez Mejías, the bullfighter:

> Blood in the streets of Santiago.
> I don't want to see it.
> Their president duly elected
> gave all he had

did what he could
to spare it.
To stop a tank, he said,
how many masses?
He didn't want to see the blood.

As we noted in Chapter 3, '¡Que no quiero verla!: I don't want to see
it!' is the constantly repeated refrain of the second section (entitled
'The Spilt Blood') of Lorca's great poem. In the Allende lament this
is linked with a direct quotation from Allende, who did not arm
the workers because he did not want to see their blood spilt. The
bullfighter theme persists in references to the military leaders who
killed him, 'the general bulls':

And in Washington they determined
your downfall
from the beginning.
And at home the princes plotted
with the bulls
to see your ending.

This echoes psalm 22 (which begins 'Why have you forsaken me?'
and was quoted by Christ on the cross):

Many bulls encompass me,
strong bulls of Bashan surround me.

There is also an echo of psalm 2:

The kings of the earth are set,
and the rulers take counsel together
against the Lord and against his anointed.

The allusion is making the point that Salvador Allende was the
legitimately elected president and at the end of the poem the desire
of the people of Chile for a government that would bring social
justice, now thwarted by this violent coup, is expressed in the (also
biblical) echo of the Advent liturgy verse and and response: *Rorate
caeli*: 'Skies, drop dew and clouds rain down the just one. Earth,
open and germinate a saviour':

badly needed
as the dew, the rain,
and as the earth is broken open
by green things pushing in spring,
you should have succeeded.

Here is an example of a 'doubledecker' allusion from the poem
'At the Gates',[8] which describes stockbrokers in the City, 'natty
youngish men, eternally thirty-one' who

. . . having commuted
daily from costly little gems
somewhere near longitude zero,
yup an English that yoyos
between yawn and snakebite,
crouch in worship of Mammon's angels
green-eyed mechanical networkers
post over land and ocean without rest
while these acolytes only
stand and wait for profit,
hum its hymns
here in their temple.

The echo of Milton's sonnet 'On his Blindness' provides a subtext
summoning Milton as Wordsworth does in *his* sonnet:

Milton! thou should'st be living at this hour:
England hath need of thee.

There are many ways of using allusion in poetry. T. S. Eliot called
the allusions with which *The Waste Land* is crammed, 'fragments
I have shored against my ruins'. Other poets may use them for
less pessimistic ends. When allusion is not so obscure as to be
unrecognisable or infuriating, or so familiar it has degenerated into
cliché, it can add in many interesting ways to a poem's density and
therefore economy.

WORDS

So much could be said about words in poems that the whole world
would not contain the books that could be written about them

(an allusion!). Here we can only deal briefly with a number of points.

Economy and Freshness

The language of poetry is economical because it says a lot in a little. A language is a living thing, constantly renewing itself. So poetry must be concise, condensed and *fresh*. No word is wasted and a poem is 'untranslatable' (Coleridge) into any other words in its own language.

At the beginning of the chapter we said the germ of a poem is a moment of intense seeing, an *insight*. This fresh seeing does not become a poem until it has been made into fresh saying. Sometimes we have no doubt that a poem or painting has arisen from a moment of genuine vision and excitement for the producer but the product strikes us as cliché. This seems to be particularly the case with a 'nature' subject, especially when it is 'picturesque'. An artist can have a very deep, real attachment to nature or a particular stretch of country and still make very bad poems or pictures of it. A good poem must say freshly what has been seen freshly; the saying must enable others to share the seeing. People can be delighted and grateful when a poem articulates what they see and feel but have never expressed, when it is 'well put'.

Each word must be selected as the best possible word not only for its rhythm and sound, but also of course for its sense and this includes its *associations*. And each word must be in the right place. Pound uses the term 'collocation' for the 'reciprocal tension that is operating between words independently of their grammatic relationship'. Each word should work hard for its place: there should be no padding, even for the sake of maintaining a rhythm. When we speak we are frequently repetitive and slack; often we may intersperse our conversation with expressions like 'um', 'er', 'sort of', 'you know', for the perfectly legitimate reason that we want to give ourselves pause to think. Poetry prunes away *redundancies* as uneconomic and stale: deadweight. It makes its impact by its concision and freshness.

This means, for example, that we need to be particularly careful with sloppy or worn-out adjectives and adverbs – 'nice, lovely, great, horrible, ghastly' are obvious examples. Paradoxically, adding 'very' can be less emphatic than an adjective on its own. Often if we use a more precise noun or verb we can dispense with qualifiers altogether.

English is particularly rich in verbs, which are of crucial importance to poetry because they are the core of the sentence, relating subject and object, persons and things to one another, usually in a dynamic way because verbs are often 'doing words'. A good choice of verbs not only adds precision but energy to the poem. A description of a woman in a kitchen will be more dynamic if it says what she is doing and to what than if it is a 'still life'. 'Next door's new kittens totter and pounce' is both more precise and more dynamic than 'sweet little kittens next door'. Even the selection of small words such as prepositions can make a considerable difference. Keats' line: 'The stars look very cold about the sky' is more interesting than 'in the sky'. When you have written a poem it is helpful to check that each word – particularly each adjective and adverb – is earning its place. It is worth checking all the plural nouns to see whether they would not sound better in the singular. It is also helpful to try crossing out the end of the poem and see if that improves it and then try crossing out the beginning of the poem and see if that improves it. It is surprising how often it does. It may be agony but ruthlessness is in order here: 'we don't want to chop you but we think you ought to go'.

However it can be economical to add a negative, because a negative expression can both introduce the idea of its opposite and deny it at the same time. For example, the refrain of the 'Ballad of Joe Hill': 'I never died, said he' both introduces the idea of 'I might have died', or 'you thought I was dead', and denies it. Likewise in the expression 'you are not alone'. What is said in the following paragraphs about words is concerned with economy either by *not wasting words* or by *increasing their density and impact*.

Poetic Vocabulary/Diction

In his 'Preface' to the *Lyrical Ballads* Wordsworth argues strongly that there should not be a special language for poetry. Poetry, he says, should be 'the real language of men in a state of vivid sensation'. Hopkins says poetry is language heightened – to any degree heightened – but not obsolete. And T. S. Eliot says 'poetry must not stray too far from the ordinary everyday language which we use and hear'. (However his own snobbishness made his use of cockney in *The Waste Land* far less convincing than that of an

EastEnders' scriptwriter.) The language we speak and hear – pruned of deadweight and redundancy – and of our own place and *time*, which is now not that of Eliot, Hopkins or Wordsworth.

There is no special 'poetic' subject matter: we cringe with Bertie Wooster when the 'poetic' Madeleine Bassett says the stars are God's daisy chain and dewdrops are fairies' tears. No human experience is unsuitable material for poetry. Likewise there is no special vocabulary or diction for poetry. We should write in the English spoken in our own time and place. We should not be needlessly obscure or flashy with foreign tags. (We should also be wary of translated foreign tags if they sound pretentious, for example, the 'liberty to dispose of oneself' may sound inspiring in French but a natural English reaction might be 'OK, show me the dustbin!') It is advisable to avoid archaic words like oft, ere, forsooth, steed, paramour, troth, verily (except in comic verse) and archaic constructions such as 'I fear lest he come'. Even two hundred years ago Wordsworth pointed out that it is not natural in English to put the adjective after the noun. We do not say 'oaks majestic' or 'kittens small'. The way to heighten language is not to dress it up in some period costume which is bound to be pastiche, but on the contrary, to seek the freshness and vigour of Lorca's 'newly created rose'. Mayakovsky says that a new time, particularly a revolutionary new time, needs a new vocabulary. In his autobiographical *Siegfried's Journey*,[9] Sassoon says that his earliest war poems were 'too noble' and he had to find a more down-to-earth language (as in 'The Dug-Out' quoted earlier) to express the reality. Poetry must speak in and for its own time and place and these strong particular roots are what give it the best chance of also speaking to others in other times and places.

The English Word Hoard

The English language has a huge vocabulary and the special richness of having Germanic and Latin and other sources. Very broadly, words for simple everyday things are more likely to be of Germanic, Anglo-Saxon, origin: man, friend, come, go, house, bread, butter, live, give, eat, kiss, sleep; and scientific or technical words are often derived from Latin or Greek: redemption, destablisation, conscientisation, oxygen. (If we learn German it sounds funny to us to hear Germanic scientific names such as 'Sauerstoff' for oxygen.) Even non-technical words deriving ultimately from Latin via Norman French tend to sound less 'homely' than words of Germanic origin. For a while before they merged, Norman French was spoken at Court and an early form of English by the people. It does not matter whether we know the origin (etymology) of a word, although browsing in an etymological dictionary is very enjoyable. But as it is preferable to write as simply and plainly as we can to say what we want, we will often feel the Anglo-Saxon derived word in everyday use is preferable to having too many more difficult or abstract Latin derived words. Usually 'cat' is preferable to 'feline creature'. But this rule is by no means universal: the whole richness of the English vocabulary is available to us to select from. If we make a fetish of using Anglo Saxon words only, the result can be folksy; if we said 'sour stuff' every time we meant oxygen we would sound like a garden gnome.

English has Few Inflections

When a language expresses changes in meaning by adding to or altering words, it is called *synthetic* (putting together). This may be done by adding bits on to the word at the beginning (prefix) or end (suffix) or altering words internally. These inflectional markers are called morphemes: the smallest meaning unit in a word. When this is done to nouns or verbs it is called inflection. We do this in English, but much less so than in some other languages. The regular verb in English has only four different inflections: walk, walks (+s), walking (+ing) and walked (+ed), whereas Spanish or German has many more. We need to add personal pronouns and many auxiliary words to mark the person, tense and so on. Likewise English regular nouns make only one change, adding 's' (with apostrophe in various places which does not affect the sound) to mark the plural or possessive. We have to make our meaning clear by the word order: 'Tim bit the dog' does not mean the same as 'The dog bit Tim'. Or we add words such as 'to', 'of' to show relationships between words. And so on. So English is the opposite of a synthetic language, it is a more *analytic* language, that is it separates things out. The ability to speak English includes knowing the possible paradigms for a sentence or phrase: understanding what the word order signifies (in the two example sentences about biting above we know who is the biter in each case), and knowing what kind of words can relate to each other in particular ways. We understand 'nonsense' verse like the 'Jabberwocky' because although many words are invented, it is following an English paradigm:

> 'Twas brillig and the slithy toves
> did gyre and gimble in the wabe;
> all mimsy were the borogoves
> and the mome raths outgrabe.

Extending the Use of Words

With the appropriate paradigm in mind, we find that one useful effect of the analytic nature of English for poetry is that *we do not have to mark words with a morpheme when we change their part of speech*. This adds a great deal of flexibility to our use of words and can make for a pleasing concision and density, or sometimes, a fruitful ambiguity.

We can use nouns as verbs: 'we dog our enemy', 'she snakes in', (how about 'I hippopotamus into the bath'?). We can use nouns as adjectives: in 'I see the moon', moon is a noun' but in 'I see the moon mouse' moon is an adjective. (In other languages the adjectival form would need an inflectional marker, making it slightly different from the noun.) Or we can speak of 'her blackbird eye', 'her marigold hair'. We can use nouns as adverbs: 'we proceed cat and mouse'. We can use verbs as nouns. Normally the verbal noun is the infinitive ('to go') or gerund ('going') But we can say 'it's all go', 'it's nothing but talk'. How about 'it's all stop'? We can use verbs as adjectives 'a stop go policy', 'A love hate affair'. We can use conjunctions as nouns 'it's all ifs and buts'. Prepositions as nouns: 'the ins and outs of it', 'between is an uncomfortable place to be'. Verb-plus-preposition as noun: 'a go between'. Prepositions as adjectives: 'the in thing', 'an out and out monetarist'. And so on. The above examples are not new coinages but illustrate how English words breed like genes in new combinations. It is up to the poet to keep producing.

Paradigm and Invention

We can have a sentence or phrase paradigm and put surprising words in it: for example, Dylan Thomas's 'a grief ago'. In this paradigm we expect a noun signifying a period of time before 'ago'. So 'A grief ago' is deviant but interesting. Other examples:

'anxiety burnt the toast' (a maker or burner of toast is usually a person or household appliance); 'it weighed a thousand groans' (groans are not usually a measure of weight); 'the mathematics of mistrust' (mathematics are usually to do with numbers); 'a piebald nightmare' (piebald usually refers to a black and white real horse, not a bad dream). 'Green is the colour of hope' is not so unusual because we understand 'green symbolises hope' but what about 'the colour of saying', 'the sound of thinking', 'the underbelly of understanding'? English has enormous possibilities for this kind of invention but we must be careful the effect is what we want, striking perhaps but not affected.

We can follow a word paradigm to invent new words. For example 'urge the mind to aftersight and foresight'. The word 'aftersight' is invented following the paradigm of 'foresight'. We can use a suffix or prefix as a paradigm (being 'synthetic' this time!). For example a North Londoner moaning about what a horrible journey it has been to the wilds of Lewisham may be rebuked: 'Don't be so northist' by analogy with racist, sexist and so on. Or Hopkins' use of the prefix 'un' to form: 'unchilding, unfathering deeps'. Hopkins is very fond of rich invented compounds:

> what wind-walks! what lovely behaviour
> of silk-sack clouds! has wilder, wilful-wavier
> meal-drift moulded ever and melted across skies?

Or: 'Though worlds of wanwood leafmeal lie'.

Handicapped Paradigms

Some English paradigms impose irritating limitations which we may discover when we find a neater solution operating in another language. Above we pointed out some of the advantages of English having few inflections. But here is an English paradigm where it is a disadvantage: 'the' plus adjective forms a plural noun – 'the rich', 'the hungry'. As in the interests of particularity poetry often prefers the singular to the plural, sometimes we may envy the ability of Spanish, for instance, to form a singular noun in this case: 'el rico' = the rich (man), 'la rica' = the rich (woman) (or if you do want the plural: 'los ricos').

Colloquial speech uses the plural as a solution to a paradigm involving the inbuilt sexism of the language in the use of the word 'man' and the pronoun 'he' to refer to the species, and in constructions like 'everyone has his own job' or 'each student is independent, he must . . . ', 'tell your child he is . . .' 'There's someone at the door. Ask him to come in.' It is cumbersome to keep repeating 'he or she', 'him or her'. In speech we overcome the assumption it is a man by using the plural: 'everyone has their own job', 'ask them to come in' and so on. But this does not solve all the problems. For example 'tell your child they are' sounds awkward but if we say, 'tell your children they are' this is not appropriate to a one-child family and do we say 'tell your children to bring their book' or 'their books' when we mean each child is to bring one book? It is a challenge to all speakers and especially poets to come up with ingenious solutions to such problems.

PUNS

Puns can be fun. Of course they are much favoured by newspaper headlines and advertising slogans. The GLC slogan for its cheap public transport campaign was 'Fares Fair'. We hear at least three messages simultaneously: the literal 'fares that are fair', the echo of the saying 'Fair's fair' – 'it's only just' – and the idea of a Fares bonanza or funfair. It was very popular. A road safety poster showing a dog standing still with front feet neatly together waiting to cross the road had the slogan: 'At the curb paws'. Apparently this did not work so well because not every accent of English pronounces 'pause' and 'paws' the same. A review title of a book about the history of contraception was 'a womb of one's own', snappy (though unattractive) because 'womb' rhymes with 'room' in Virginia Woolf's *A Room of One's Own* (a punning allusion). An advertisement for Vladivar vodka has the slogan 'Vladi good vodka!' said by a glamorous Russian-looking woman – a witty rendering of her enticing foreign accent.

Children have pun-loving periods and there are plenty of awful ones published in joke books. For example: 'Irish stew in the name of the law!' Or two old favourites:

> 'My wife has gone to the West Indies.'
> 'Jamaica?'
> 'No she went of her own free will.'

The god of thunder bestrode his mighty war horse. 'I'm Thor!'
    he cried.
The horse answered: 'You forgot your thaddle, thilly!'

Poetry that is not intending to be comic should use puns with discretion, because they may provide a cheap distraction from the poem's purpose. In his 'Art Poétique' Verlaine advises:

> Fuis du plus loin la pointe assassine,
> l'esprit cruel et le rire impur.

> Keep well away from the killing pun,
> cruel wit and the sniggering laugh.

WORD ASSOCIATION

On a scale ranging between (P) particular and (Q) universal, poetry starts at (P). It does not then move away from this towards (Q) but spreads *across* the range, *covering it* like mercury up a thermometer. And if we think of writing as having a whole range of purposes between (A) recording speech and (B) encoding ideas (ultimately to the point of something like a mathematical formula), poetry begins near the (A) end (although it eliminates the redundancies of natural speech). Likewise, it does not then move away from this towards (B) but spreads across the whole range. The particular does not exclude the universal but embodies it and although we can pinpoint a more or less precise meaning for a word – which may be as precise as our mathematical formula at the ultimate point (B) – in poetry the aim is not to 'purify' a word of anything but a single literal meaning but the opposite. A word accrues many *associations* both as an individual word and in the way it is grouped with other words.

In previous chapters we noted how the rhythm or sound of words may have *associations* for us. Obviously the same goes for the sense of words. In a poem – which provides a *context* – the rhythm, sound and sense of the words operate together in a complex interplay of associations which all contribute to the poem's total meaning. As we noted above, poems may *allude* to other poems or texts, in any degree from full quotation to a faint echo. This is one kind of association. But the associations of words or phrases obviously have a much broader scope than allusion to other poems. For example, we laugh when someone calls their cat Rover, because we associate the name with a dog. Every speaker has a rich store of memories of the ways in which they have heard words or phrases used up to the point when they read the poem. These are the word's associations. Out of this mass, which will be partly shared with others in the same country, city, or family, and partly personal to each individual, poets can choose to *foreground* certain associations by the way they select and relate the words in the poem. One of the main ways of doing this is by the use of *figurative language*.

FIGURATIVE LANGUAGE

Metaphor and Simile

We said earlier that poetry appeals first to the senses through *images*. These images may be not only a clear evocation of a particular object in the world but also a *comparison*. Some of the examples given above implied a comparison. When we say 'her blackbird eye' referring to a girl, we mean she has an eye like a blackbird's: perhaps suggesting bright, observant, steady. Her eye is *associated* with a blackbird's. When we say 'her marigold hair' we mean her hair is like a marigold, a flower with many vigorous yellow petals. This is called a *metaphor*. A metaphor does not have to be a noun: in examples given above 'snakes in' 'hippopotamus into', or in 'don't keep rabbiting on', the metaphor is a verb. If we express the comparison explicitly using a word such as 'like' – 'my love is like a red red rose' – this is called a *simile*. Note that the comparison has to be like in some respect but not in every respect. We mean her hair is like a marigold *in some ways* or my love is like a red rose *in some way*. Simile is an overt comparison and metaphor a covert comparison. Metaphor is more compact than simile and therefore often preferred in the interests of concentration. But we may choose a simile because we want to make explicit in what respect one thing is compared to another: 'I wandered *lonely* as a cloud'.

In the metaphor 'green is the colour of hope' we mean hope is like green (or some green things) in some way: the underlying suggestion is a comparison to the seasons in a country where things die in winter but unfailingly sprout green again in spring.

Libby Houston's short poem 'For the Record'[10] is made by its simile:

> saw for a second
> neck and neck with us
> on the motorway
> some vole
> going like one fur
> cylinder –
>
> no chance!

Or here is another, apt if disgusting simile from her poem 'The Quarry':

> A light touch –
> two flies like friends, their heads together,
> feeding from the wound.

Jane Duran's 'Rabah Saïd'[11] doing his wonderful belly dance in a cold Swedish flat finishes with two climactic metaphors:

> gliding, eddying
> across the marine snows of Sweden:
> a sandstorm at dawn,
> his red shirt – banners.

We use metaphor and simile not just to make a neat enlightening comparison for the mind but also to help express *feeling*. For example if a woman says 'Forbes is a toad' and 'Jeff is a lamb', we assume she prefers Jeff. Metaphor and simile are fundamentally important to poetry both because they deal in particular images and because they bring the added concentration of *making connections*.

We noted above that metaphors like 'carpet bombing' or 'surgical strike' can deceive or lull our imagination by *distracting* it from the reality being described. It is the poet's task to challenge these *euphemisms*. And in general, metaphors and all figures of speech can wear out and become clichés – which are fossilised poetry, i.e. they are dead. For example: 'ice cold', 'sun kissed', 'rock hard', 'pure as the driven snow', 'stinking rich' . . . They do not strike the senses, so they are not only pointless and wasteful but may even actually numb us.

But if new-minted metaphors are like abstruse crossword puzzle clues they may operate only at a very superficial level. A poem like 'A Martian Sends a Postcard Home' which gave its name to the 'Martian School' of poetry may appeal greatly to the riddle-loving nine-year-old but is very limited in feeling and vision.

Other Figures of Speech

Besides metaphor and simile there are many other 'figures of speech' that can be used in poetry. We cannot give a complete list and refer the reader to any good dictionary of literary terms.[12] Here we give a dozen or so examples.

Metonymy means 'using the name of one thing for that of something else with which it is associated'. For example 'E wing held well' does not mean that this particular wing of the prison building stood firmly but that the prisoners in this wing held out a long time in the prison riot. 'Our street hasn't paid the poll tax' means the people in our street. (Likewise Tennyson's 'kneeling hamlet'.) Metonymy is particularly useful, for example, for summoning loyalties: 'Come on, Manchester!' Or, conversely, for dissociating yourself from another group: 'What a very Hampstead remark!'

Synecdoche is similar. It applies the part to the whole. For example: 'All hands on deck!' It can be used abusively, as in referring to women as 'skirt'.

Symbolism: metaphor and metonymy may also be *symbolic*. For example in Keats' 'bright star would I were steadfast as thou art', the star is not just a metaphor but also a symbol of steadfastness, constancy. A skull (which has a natural connection with death) is a metonymic symbol. When symbols become conventional and worn out they do not have much poetic energy unless they are used in a fresh way.

Allegory combines a number of different symbols into a totality, probably a story. For example in the *Pilgrim's Progress* the characters whom the hero Christian meets (Mr Great-heart, the Giant Despair) and the places on his journey (Vanity Fair, the Slough of Despond) are all symbolic. It would be possible to read *Pilgrim's Progress* just for the story.

Personification: a quality may be embodied or symbolised in a person, such as Mr Great-Heart in the *Pilgrim's Progress*. Or when in *Piers Plowman* Mercy and Truth meet together (fulfilling the psalm),

Mercy is 'a full benign burde and buxom of speech'. Later they meet Righteousness who is sharp-tongued and snaps: 'Why ravest thou or art thou right drunk?'

In a modern example 'Daphne'[13] by Kathleen McPhilemy, mythical Daphne, now a rooted laurel tree, speaks as a housewife and mother. In this personification she is also a symbol (of being 'tied down') and the whole poem is an allegory:

> When the wind blew through the thicket
> her branches ached, she groaned, her roots tightened;
> she held her place in the forest
> at least she knew where she was

Pathetic Fallacy means assuming a connection between our own mood and surrounding nature. The storm in Jane Eyre's heart is matched by a real Yorkshire storm. You are happy in love and the sun shines. It may be a fallacy that our moods affect nature and the weather but it is not a fallacy that nature and weather affect our moods. For the last few days London has been frozen, covered in snow and my kitchen sink blocked. I found myself unable to write anything however hard I tried. Last night there was a slight thaw, the sink unblocked itself and this morning I am writing this!

Zeugma means yoking two unlikely partners in a single phrase: 'He arrives with flowers and urgent political action'. 'She went home in fury and a taxi'. The effect tends to be comic.

Ellipse means leaving out words usually regarded as grammatically essential in the sentence. The effect is telegraphic: 'Have squared boss. Arriving Paris tonight.'

Oxymoron is the combination of two usually incompatible things. Sometimes this is done to express (perhaps exaggerated and clichéd) extremes of feeling. Shakespeare has fun sending up Romeo's romantic pose of love for Rosaline (before he becomes really involved – with Juliet): 'O heavy lightness! Serious vanity! . . . Feather of lead, bright smoke, cold fire, sick health! . . . ' Other examples of oxymoron are the 'young fogey' or in contrast, Nicaraguan revolutionaries 'armed to the teeth with tenderness'.

Paradox is related to oxymoron and means making a contradictory assertion: 'the dead are alive'. In a paradox the statement turns out not to be contradictory because, for example, the dead are said to be alive in a particular way which is not incompatible with them also being dead.

Hyperbole means exaggeration. For example:

> As fair art thou my bonny lass,
> so deep in love am I:
> that I will love thee still my dear
> till all the seas gang dry.

Here the exaggeration is used to protest the strength of the poet's passion. Obviously conventional hyperboles such as 'he's got tons of money' will not have much force in a poem because they are the opposite of precise and particular.

Litotes means the contrary to hyperbole: rhetorical understatement. For example: 'it was not awfully comfortable in the trenches.' Some people think of litotes as 'being British'.

Irony takes various forms. In dramatic irony we the audience know something that at least one of the characters in a play (or dramatic poem) does not. An 'irony of fate' would fall upon a person who survived a long dangerous expedition through the jungle and the day she arrived home safely was run over by a taxi. Irony related to sarcasm is a matter of tone; it criticises through an expression of praise or neutrality. Someone does something very cruel to you and you say : 'That was kind of him.' A rich man is acquitted of fraud and embezzlement and a poor man sent to prison for a social security fraud involving £100: 'That's justice for you!'

The quality of a poem will depend a great deal on the poet's skill in inventing and placing metaphors and other figures of speech. Used successfully they make a poem more enjoyable, increase its density and therefore economy. Worn out ways of saying things are wasteful and counterproductive. The language we speak and hear but with an economy, intensity and 'a sensation of freshness wholly unknown' is what gives a poem the energy that is 'eternal delight'.

NOTES

1. Translated in *Nicaraguan New Time*.
2. In *Witness to Magic*.
3. In *Making Cocoa for Kingsley Amis* (London: Faber, 1986).
4. From lecture on 'The Theory and Function of the Duende' printed as appendix to Lorca, *Selected Poems* translated by J. L. Gili (London: Penguin, 1960).

5. 'Thoughts about the Person from Porlock' and 'The Word' are both in Stevie Smith, *Collected Poems* (London: Penguin, 1975).
6. John Heath-Stubbs, *Collected Poems*.
7. 'The Death of Allende' is in *Keeping Heart*.
8. 'At the Gates' by D. L. is in *Camden Voices 1978-90*.
9. *Siegfried's Journey* by Siegfried Sassoon (London: Faber and Faber, 1945).
10. 'For the Record' and 'The Quarry' by Libby Houston are in *Necessity* (Nottingham: Slow Dancer, 1988).
11. 'The Wonderful Belly Dance of Rabah Saïd' by Jane Duran is in *Camden Voices 1978-90*.
12. Martin Gray, *A Dictionary of Literary Terms* (Harlow: Longman, 1984); Chris Baldick, *The Concise Oxford Dictionary of Literary Terms* (Oxford: Oxford University Press, 1990); J. A. Cudden, *A Dictionary of Literary Terms* (London: Penguin, 1976).
13. 'Daphne' is in *Witness to Magic*.

5

Poetry in Society

What benefit canst thou, or all thy tribe
to the great world?

Keats, 'The Fall of Hyperion'

The last chapter discussed the content of poetry. In this chapter we
consider some of the functions of poetry in the society to which
it is addressed: its audience. All societies have had poets and it
may occur to us to wonder why. A language is the main way
in which a society expresses itself and coheres through understanding. In the last chapter we said that a language is a living
thing that grows and must constantly renew itself. Poetry which
renews by using it in fresh, unautomatic and unpredictable ways
is the heart of any language's struggle to live vigorously and
maintain a high quality of life throughout the social body in which
it circulates. In his 'Preface' to the *Lyrical Ballads* Wordsworth
says:

> Poetry is the most philosophic of all writing: its object is
> truth . . . not standing upon external testimony, but carried
> alive into the heart by passion . . . The poet writes under one
> restriction only, namely the necessity of giving immediate pleas-
> ure . . . The end of poetry is to produce excitement in co-existence
> with an overbalance of pleasure . . . We have no sympathy but
> what is propagated by pleasure . . . wherever we sympathise
> with pain it will be found that the sympathy is produced and
> carried on by subtle combinations with pleasure.

Plato did not want poets in his republic because he said they told
lies. Actually, as John-Heath Stubbs' poem 'Plato and the Waters of
the Flood'[1] shows, it is the other way round. The 'republic' with its
politicians and 'establishment' tells the lies. Plato

96

> reared a republic in the mind
> where only noble lies
> reign; he expelled the poets . . .

The poets with their *subversive* truth are exiled, pushed under-ground: they articulate the unconscious, their knowing is dangerous, even more their speaking, their *soothsaying*. But society needs them because it needs to listen to the truth about itself. The poem ends:

> When will you rise again,
> ten horned, seven-headed seraphim
> out of your abyss,
> against the beautiful Republic,
> nor tamed by Plato's kiss?

Part of a poet's function in society must be to *break silences* and *unmask lies*, particularly of established powers. In the previous chapter we noted some wartime lying by the use of such metaphors as 'carpet bombing' and 'surgical strike'. This language has now become *automatic* and it is the poet's job to resist the 'lethal automaton', not just in wartime but in a society's everyday life – by telling the truth. The function of soothsayers and prophets is not only to 'see' the future but to 'speak out' the truth about the present. A present-day society is no less likely to worship idols than a 'primitive' one. Idols have been defined as false gods who demand and feed on death. They do not need to legitimate themselves because if you touch them they kill you. Idols often wear masks face-painted with lies, slogans and automatic language. The struggle to smash these idols of death and transform the world so that all may have abundant life has been compared to a poem or song; 'the highest form of song is the struggle' is the modest motto of the famous revolutionary singers Los de Palacagüina. This does not mean all poems and songs have to be about 'the struggle'. On the other hand, as we saw, the slogan 'Keep politics out of poetry' (or schools, health etc.) masks a determination to maintain an unjust status quo. Explicitly or implicitly poetry must break ranks from the lethal automaton. Poetry may contribute directly to the struggle either by *articulating our desires*: 'seeing' a transformed future or by 'speaking out' about the present, as forms of *encouragement*. But it would be too narrow a view to confine poetry's role to this. Poetry itself is a struggle to be truthful and a form of abundant life. Thus as well as sometimes contributing directly, poetry is also part of what the struggle is *for*. Poetry on its own does not change the world enough but in so far as the unmasking of idols is *language* work, this specifically concerns poets.

If poetry rises again out of the abyss, this means it must have gone down into it and poets who do not 'take the depths' – of their society and their own unconscious – 'harrow hell' – will not rise again with anything of value to offer. They may even become part of the system of 'noble lies' (and perhaps do very well out of it). In the story of the harrowing of hell in *Piers Plowman* Christ (the Word) challenges Lucifer (the father of lies) at the gates of hell:

> Thou art Doctor of Death, drink that thou madest!
> I that am Lord of Life, love is my drink,
> and for that drink today I died upon earth.

Paul says of the harrowing of hell:[2]

> Therefore it is said, 'When he ascended he led captivity captive and gave gifts to humanity'. In saying, 'He ascended,' what does it mean but that he had also descended into the lowest parts of the earth?

In the section on poetry's scope in the last chapter, we said no arbitrary limitations should be placed on it in the name of 'taste', or fashion. Poetry's scope is all experience, from the most humdrum and daily to the depths and heights of our human reality and imagination – 'hell' and 'heaven'. Its starting point stands firmly in its own time and place. It has a duty to *them*. As Kathleen McPhilemy says in her poem 'Nawroz: the Kurdish New Year, 21st March 1985', which we have already looked at technically:[3]

> The difficulty's in honouring the truth:
> to match the shifting inner outer worlds
> to find the words, transgress what friends expect.
> We need a language as subtle-sour as tears
> that stung to see the miners sent ahead
> defeated banner high, to lead the Londoners . . .
>
> This spring belongs to the refugees and miners
> to Kurds who celebrate in a new language
> their own story of Azdahak and Kawa

an end of tyranny, a hope of freedom.
Words come round again; the letter comes
that orders deportation. Very subtle now
in all the shades of their defilement
the words are ours and witness to the time.

POETRY IN THE PAST

Every society has produced poets and many scholars have written about them, more than enough for a lifetime's reading. Choose what attracts you most. Here we only have space to mention a couple of examples of poets in past societies. Two things make an obvious difference to poetry's function in a society: reading and printing. In a society where most people cannot read, poetry is recited or sung to an audience for whom this is a communal experience. In a society where many people can read, and even more so when printing makes books more freely available, a poet's work may be read by an individual alone with a book. This will probably affect the way poets write. Both these ways of absorbing poetry are practised in Britain today and there is considerable debate about their respective merits.

Christopher Hampton's *The Ideology of the Text*[4] gives some examples of poets functioning in their own societies and is particularly illuminating about Milton and Blake. Here we can simply remind the reader of their historical context and offer a quotation from each poet for consideration in that context. Milton wrote his great epic with the significant title *Paradise Lost* at a time of revolutionary upheaval in England – the 'Commonwealth' – followed by the restoration of the monarchy, which for Milton meant a hope of paradise lost:

That a nation should be so valorous and courageous to win their liberty in the field, and when they have won it, should be so heartless and unwise in their counsels, as not to know how to use it, value it, what to do with it, or with themselves; but after ten or twelve years prosperous war and contestation with tyranny, basely and besottedly to run their necks again into the yoke which they have broken, and prostitute all the fruits of their victory for nought at the feet of the vanquished, besides our loss of glory, and such an example as kings or tyrants never yet had the like to boast of, will be an ignominy if it befall us, that never yet befell any nation possessed of their liberty . . .

Blake wrote at a time of revolution in France, industrial revolution in England and war between the two countries. He engaged with the society of his time, denouncing its repression and exploitation in his *Songs of Experience*. In his 'London':

> I wander through each chartered street,
> near where the chartered Thames does flow,
> and mark in every face I meet
> marks of weakness, marks of woe . . .
>
> How the chimney sweepers cry
> every blackening church appals
> and the hapless soldier's sigh
> runs in blood down palace walls . . .

Blake's long much more difficult poem *Jerusalem* is about the struggle to build the ideal city. Jerusalem is London (the City, *polis*, ultimately humanity), a London transformed from the grim realities of the London of his day (and in many respects still very much our day). Part of the poem's power lies in its invocation of London names.

> The fields from Islington to Marybone,
> to Primrose Hill and Saint John's Wood,
> were builded over with pillars of gold,
> and there Jerusalem's pillars stood . . .
>
> Pancras and Kentish Town repose
> among her golden pillars high,
> among her golden arches which
> shine upon the starry sky.
>
> The Jew's Harp House and the Green Man,
> the ponds where boys to bathe delight,
> the fields of cows by Willan's farm,
> shine in Jerusalem's pleasant sight . . .
>
> Is this thy soft family love,
> thy cruel patriarchal pride,

planting thy family alone,
destroying all the world beside? . . .

A man's worst enemies are those
of his own house and family;
and he who makes his law a curse,
by his own law shall surely die.

In my exchanges every land
shall walk and mine in every land
mutual shall build Jerusalem
both heart in heart and hand in hand.

The paradise lost by Adam and Eve was a garden. Blake's heaven on earth was a city. These two images of paradise sometimes conflict. For example in Marvell's 'The Garden' paradise is very definitely *not* the city. In various relationships they recur and interact again and again in English literature. Both images are biblical and in the final vision of *Revelation* city and garden become one:

> The river of the water of life, bright as crystal . . . flows through the middle of the street of the city; also beside the river the tree of life with its twelve kinds of fruit, yielding its fruit each month; and the leaves of the tree for the healing of nations.[5]

Taking an example with a strong emphasis on the former, the joys of nature, we glance briefly now at one rather fascinating story of the poetry of the past having effects, or perhaps repercussions is the word, over several generations.

POETRY'S REPERCUSSIONS: A SOMERSET EXAMPLE

The poets Coleridge and Wordsworth spent their crucial years 1797–8 living in the Quantocks in Somerset. Coleridge's 'Ancient Mariner' set out from the nearby little port of Watchet. During these two years they often walked as far as Lynton either alone, together or with friends, discussing poetry. 'The Rime of the Ancient Mariner', one of the poems to be published in the *Lyrical Ballads* and the whole idea of this joint work, were discussed on one of these walks. Coleridge wrote 'Kubla Khan' at Ash Farm directly above tiny Culbone Church, which lies on the coastal path between Porlock and Lynton, and was interrupted by a 'person from Porlock'.[6] Wordsworth composed his 'Tintern Abbey' on a walking tour in July 1798 and returned home to Somerset to include it in the *Lyrical Ballads*, which was already at the printers and published that September.

'Tintern Abbey' contains Wordsworth's passionate credo as a 'worshipper of nature':

> I cannot paint
> what then I was. The sounding cataract
> haunted me like a passion; the tall rock,
> the mountain, and the deep and gloomy wood,
> their colours and their forms, were then to me
> an appetite: a feeling and a love . . .

Now, he says:

> . . . I have learnt
> to look on nature, not as in the hour
> of thoughtless youth, but hearing oftentimes
> the still, sad music of humanity,
> nor harsh nor grating, though of ample power
> to chasten and subdue. And I have felt
> a presence that disturbs me with the joy
> of elevated thoughts . . .

That is why he is:

> . . . well pleased to recognise
> in nature and the language of the sense
> the anchor of my purest thoughts, the nurse,
> the guide, the guardian of my heart, and soul
> of all my moral being.

The Acland[7] family owned vast acres of land in Somerset near Porlock, including Horner Water, one of many steep scrub-oak wooded combes with streams rushing down to twist along the bottom, and the open moors of Exmoor with Dunkery Beacon its highest point. The tenth baronet the 'Great Sir Thomas' (from 1808 to 1871) used to walk up to Selworthy Beacon (above Porlock on the seaward side) after Sunday church at Selworthy with his friend the rector and his children and grandchildren 'instructing them in the love of nature and . . . poetry', as the inscription reads in the memorial hut erected on the way up to the Beacon. His belief in the moral power of nature owed a good deal to the poetry of Wordsworth and Coleridge. A memorial in Selworthy Church to this 9h Thomas and his son the eleventh baronet reads:

> They were deeply attached to this valley and devoted to the welfare of its inhabitants. Animated by a strong affection for their hill country home, they constantly strove to render the natural beauty of its surroundings more available to their neighbours and to visitors from afar.

This tradition was continued by Sir Thomas, the twelfth baronet, who during the First World War leased all his Exmoor lands to the National Trust for 500 years. His son Francis commented after a glorious ride: 'It's really a magnificent stretch of country. Jolly to think it'll all be national!' Sir Richard Acland, the fifteenth baronet, became a socialist in the thirties, leading his own 'Common Wealth' party during the Second World War and advocating common ownership for moral reasons. He gave all his land to the National Trust in 1944. It is heartening that:

> the guide, the guardian of my heart, and soul
> of all my moral being

led this ancestral great landowner, developing a family tradition going back to Wordsworth and Coleridge's time, not to believe in 'planting thy family alone' and to give away the stunningly beautiful country that had inspired the two poets at the peak of their powers, so that the public can enjoy it today.

QUESTIONS FOR POETRY IN BRITAIN TODAY

A little poetry handbook is not the place to give a full scale survey of the poets active in Britain today or to attempt to rank or map them.

The following paragraphs look briefly at the current scene in poetry performing and publishing and some of the issues being debated. In this section I have avoided mentioning names of individual contemporary poets because my object here is not criticism but to offer a rough sketch of the whole area, outlining certain salient features, in the hope that it may be of use, especially to new explorers.

We said that a poet's task is to see and to tell the truth and that no human experience is unsuitable material for poetry. Beginning not with truth in the abstract but the particular truth you see and feel from where you are in your own body: perhaps falling in love, losing a tooth, quarrelling over the washing up, dealing with grease, taking a cold plunge, itching as seawater dries on your skin, sunbathing, stroking a cat, drinking white wine . . .

One power of the body is to use various organs to speak. This is partly what is meant by a poet's voice: the sound of that person's particularity. Perhaps the most important development in poetry in Britain since the sixties is that now we hear voices coming from many more places than before: more female, working class, black, unemployed voices, more Cockney, Caribbean, Scouse, Geordie, Somerset accents – to mention but a few – than in the past. These voices both speak for themselves and out of experience shared with a group. The way individual poets relate to their group varies. For example some women call themselves 'women poets' and write mainly about exclusively female experience; others see themselves as poets who are women and write as women but not exclusively about 'women's subjects'.

This poetry – which obviously varies a good deal in quality – is very important not only for the individual or group gaining a voice but also for the society as a whole, which is hearing a wide range of human experience and points of view articulated in poetry, instead of just the limited experience of a (mainly white male) 'elite'. When we say experience we do not mean that all this verse must be confessional and about the individual's personal life; we also mean the point of view *from which* the poet looks at the world. We said that one of poetry's tasks in society is to break silences and unmask lies. There are also silences and lies of *jargon, familiarity, complicity,* less than half-truths when a situation is described only from 'above' rather than 'below'. If an 'establishment' says 'that's the way it is' in anodyne terms designed to maintain a status quo, the outsider, the *other* needs to say in fresh language: 'but this is the way it feels to me, us' and therefore that is not the way it *should* be. Silences are broken, lies unmasked by fresh language from a different perspective – through experience and/or imaginative sympathy – so that a prescriptive and repressive 'that's the way it is' becomes a *descriptive* 'telling it how it feels', which may be a summons to change. Poetry cannot fulfil its soothsaying (telling the truth) and prophetic (speaking out) task in society without these 'other' voices. It is also good for poets to be genuinely interested in other people and not just themselves! Sometimes to try and write about or from another – perhaps oppressed or voiceless – person's point of view. But just as oppressed people ultimately have to take their own freedom, they also – as an essential part of this liberation – need to find their own voice. The better the poetry, the greater the power to 'produce excitement in co-existence with an overbalance of pleasure', arouse sympathy that is 'propagated by pleasure' and ensure that their truth is 'carried alive into the heart by passion'.

A poet's voice is seldom at its clearest when her or his work is 'spontaneous blurting'. Although some poems come all at once as a single 'inspiration' and the poet does not need to change anything, many poets work hard on a poem before they are satisfied with it. Paradoxically the poet's voice sounds clearer in the well-made poem with the qualities we have been discussing in previous chapters: 'spontaneity' is often a hard-won achievement. So what exactly do we mean by a poet's voice and how do you get one? You have to make poems which satisfy you and have your particular sound. You have to make poems which satisfy other people so that they hear you. 'There is no such thing as a private language.' This is not an easy task and is most likely to succeed with years of struggle and dedication. Poets who arrive at a reading with 'something I just thought of in the bus' are seldom enjoyed; their audience often itches for rotten eggs.

Perhaps the first thing to remember about a voice is that it is a physical thing, a bodily power. You cannot get a voice unless you use it, read or recite your poems *out loud*. This requires as much skill and practice as writing the poem. The speaking voice also conveys much more information about the poet's particularity than the printed word: your voice is an individual voice but also the voice of a particular sex, region, social group, generation.

Poetry serves society when it makes available all this wealth of intractable particularity. Each true voice contributes. Gaining

a voice not only empowers an individual or group through self-
expression giving the possibility of being heard. It also *builds the
City*. A society in which individuals or groups have no voice is
repressive and in good poetry a voice is most itself. 'The end of
poetry is to produce excitement in co-existence with an overbalance
of pleasure'. When a voice is heard with pleasure this creates
mutuality. We said earlier that when we hear an excellent poem
performed with power (or *duende*) part of what we feel is love.
Love is 'builder of cities', not just in the literal sense that lovers
tend to have babies, but because it joins people. Blake's Jerusalem
is London – and also 'every land' . Building a city involves many
skilled trades. A good poet is a liberated voice joining in the *language
work* that

> mutual shall build Jerusalem
> both heart in heart and hand in hand.

The primary material of poetry is the spoken word. Remember
Hopkins: 'Poetry the darling child of speech, of lips and spoken
utterance . . . till it is spoken it is not performed, it does not perform, it is not itself.' Listening to poetry is often an underdeveloped
skill in a literate culture; people who cannot read are better at it. It
is a skill we need to develop through much practice. Thus a poet
requires at least three skills: the skill to make poems, the skill to
speak them out loud and the skill to listen to others.

Over the last few decades there have been many poetry readings
of all kinds in Britain. Format, venue and everything else vary a
great deal. Some poets appear not to agree that the spoken word
is poetry's primary material. They may self-importantly shuffle
through an ill-prepared heap of papers or worse, pile of slim
volumes – and eventually mumble a number of poems. This is
presumably meant as an invitation to read their books! At the other
extreme there are 'performance poets' or 'ranters' who may deliver
their work superbly – without a text – and be very entertaining.
Sometimes they may be so instantly accessible that you enjoy it
while it lasts but have no urge to go back to it and if you do
happen to see it printed somewhere you feel disappointed, even
cheated, because there does not seem to be much there. Other poets
are good performers, use their voice well and their poems 'get to'
you, give you 'a buzz'. You feel excited, moved, troubled perhaps.
Something touches you and you feel you have got hold of something

but that there is much more that has eluded you. So you want to hear the poem again, perhaps read it and mull over it. If a good poet reads for half an hour it is impossible to take everything in. Perhaps your concentration span cannot encompass more than three or four poems. But you are attracted and you want more. This is where print comes in. Then perhaps after you have absorbed more of the poems in solitary communion, you may want to hear them out loud again.

There are hundreds of poetry 'venues' in Britain today. There is the market venue where 'we don't just put on readings now: we do promotions', an embarrassment to many poets. But a cheerful multiplicity of readings or gigs take place in 'voice boxes', barns, universities, towers, colleges, pubs, clubs, cafes, churches, halls, community centres, restaurants, theatres, cellars, assembly rooms . . . and outdoors in streets, parks, squares, gardens, cloisters, porches, on steps, piers, beaches, cliffs . . . They may be picnics, festivals, protests, benefits, gigs for specific occasions such as the Twenty-four-hour Anti nuclear Marathon on the steps of St Martins in the Fields or the Water reading in the Conway Hall when our water was sold. This was an interesting example of a reading where everyone was invited to bring poems about water and most of the poems did not specifically address the political issue of the sale but were about water in every aspect of our lives on earth, some very beautiful poems, and the occasion 'added up'. All over the country people meet in poetry workshops, where they try out their poems on one another and discuss poetry. Some of these workshops are for specific groups: students in a college, women only, black writers. Workshops are often linked with performance venues. There are regular venues which invite a guest poet each time as well as 'poets from the floor'. The best of these venues are patent examples of how poetry helps build the City. Regularly meeting, speaking, listening, discerning – some of the guest poets may have a very high reputation – the participants create a poetic community, a sign in miniature of the City. Or, to put it the other way round, such venues not only offer the opportunity for poetry to perform but are a meeting point combatting some of the hideous loneliness and alienation that remote rural areas, quiet suburbs and big cities in their current state may inflict on their inhabitants. In this case poetry not only produces pleasure but diminishes pain. At a good poetry reading, above all when the *duende* is present, something happens, something is *done*, a wave of positive and convivial human energy is released, so that those present may feel afterwards: Didn't our hearts burn when we heard?

There is a great deal of discussion in Britain today about the relative merits of hearing poetry performed or reading it in books. This sometimes heated debate (deriving its energy from other fundamental disagreements about poetry and society and possibly from a form of 'class war') often becomes shadow boxing. It seems obvious that listening to poetry spoken aloud and reading poetry in silence are both valuable activities with different functions. Poetry books are records of sounds, like a musical score. Never to hear poetry out loud would be like never hearing music out loud. But poetry consists of words and a poet often wants to say something too complex to be taken in at a single hearing. We may have favourite poems in books that we go back to again and again throughout life. Learning by heart is good but we cannot learn everything.

Book and magazine publishers act as filters for poetry seeking to be read. Opening, sniffing and patting a well-produced brand new book of poems by a poet you like and settling down to read is a delicious pleasure. This is not the place to go into detailed opinions of publishers, magazines or individual poets; readers must judge for themselves. The biggest and best known publishing houses are more likely to get their books reviewed in the best-funded and established magazines as well as in the national daily, weekly and Sunday papers, which review a strictly limited amount of poetry. This often has the effect of a closed circle, which exasperated outsiders sometimes refer to as a 'mafia'. But it should be noted that the editors in these well established publishing firms and magazines do not necessarily have the best poetic judgment. They may be driven by market forces, and therefore publish the 'safe bet'; they may be interested in maintaining a *status quo* and safeguarding what they regard as an elite to the exclusion of unfamiliar, perhaps disturbing voices; they may limit poetry's scope in order to conform with established canons of 'good taste' – by definition conformist; they may be *part* of the system of 'noble lies' instead of challenging it; they may simply evade 'the difficulty in honouring the truth, to match the shifting inner outer worlds', fail to bear witness and worship the idols instead of unmasking them. Indeed, they may not even see any of this as poetry's task, preferring it to be 'art for art's sake'.

The 'market' view of poetry seeks out likely prospects to promote and then worries that if they let too many through the market will be flooded. This is the opposite of a view of poetry as liberated voices contributing to the City. The market model is allied to the ethos of the poetry competition. Many competitions are money-making ventures charging an entrance fee of several pounds per poem. Out of sometimes thousands of entries judges are appointed to pick the winner, who receives a prize. The process is bound to be a bit like a lottery especially when the same judge does not read all the poems and sub-sifters are appointed to weed out the 'no-hopers' (who lose their bet). Competition winners may then get offers of publication. Some people enter competitions for a bit of fun as others might have a flutter on the Grand National (I would prefer the latter). Perhaps the most uncomfortable thing about competitions is that they promote a view of poetry in society in which a few are 'winners' and all the rest are 'losers'. Poetry is no longer a tool for conviviality or builder of cities but each private poet hopes to beat all the rest.

Some editors regard poetry merely as a form of entertainment – 'play is very important'. What matters most for them is that a poem should be 'done well'. It does matter that it should be done well but it also matters *what* is done. Accused of frivolity and failure to witness to the time a 'marketeer' or an 'arts for art's saker' will reply that they *are* witnessing because this is what the times are like. But there is a difference between being a *phenomenon* of the times and a conscious witness and seer willing to 'take the depths'. (These latter may in their turn be dismissed as over-earnest preachers and producers of 'not art'. And certainly it is not impossible for the most well intentioned poet to be a bad one.)

Many readers of poetry feel frustrated at how unexciting and limited they find much 'establishment' poetry. This is where they expect to discover the best new poetry being written and do not. Many writers of poetry feel frustrated at constant rejections by 'establishment' publishers and magazines. Some think this may be because the poetry they write is not good enough (and the question should certainly be asked!) Others decide they disagree with these editors and look for outlets elsewhere. (Of course there is also a factor of arbitrariness and luck: whom you happen to know, meet, marry . . . Perhaps there always will be.)

These frustrations are the main reason for the proliferation of small presses and magazines, greatly helped by the spread of wordprocessors and desktop publishing. The *Catalogue* of the Association of Little Presses, the *Small Press Year Book* and the invaluable

Poetry Listing (not confined to small press output) list a huge number and variety of presses and publications. Some of these small presses have now become quite large and some are one person's self-publishing. Some poets publish themselves in preference to seeking a publisher because they like to control their own books. The Poetry Library on the South Bank publishes a list of small magazines (by no means exhaustive). As so much material is thus being published, besides printing poems, these little magazines have a useful function in *reviewing* poetry books and pamphlets ignored by the national press. Readers will become acquainted with the tastes of a particular editor or reviewer and this is a help in deciding what poets they will look out for in the future or avoid, because obviously no one can read everything.

Perhaps one more thing we might consider is why children usually love poetry, beginning with rhymes and songs, and why it often gets 'knocked out of them' at around puberty. Perhaps this happens less often than in the past because many excellent teachers have tried hard to see that it doesn't. Teachers who probably encourage children to write poems too. All power to these young poets – children are an important social group needing a voice – and to their teachers. Perhaps we should also look at it the other way round. What do children have which we as adults often lack? Obviously as adults we must write as adults and eschew a sugary 'innocence' or naivety. But if poetry is to help build Jerusalem – heaven on earth – the 'city of found identity and fullness of being together', the city of liberated voices where justice and humanity reign, perhaps as we have heard, in some way we also need to become like children in order to join in.

Finally, although there are many poets in Britain today – and granted that poetry has a humanising and prophetic role in society – a disturbing thought does nevertheless occur. Poets may speak out but does our society as a whole take much notice? Does its 'repressive tolerance', together with the economic clout of the marketable, the sheer volume of the complacent, bland and accommodating chorus, entrench the idols and drown the small voices of imagination and subversion? Is this merely a 'civilised' form of censorship to ensure there is no change in the fair weather plain sailing for the powers-that-be, however exploitative, and foul weather for the poor? Of course poetry cannot change the world on its own, its job is to speak and there is no God to back up prophets with thunderbolts. Poets speaking are part of the people's own action to liberate themselves, but in Britain why do the people often seem to be wearing earplugs? Yes, thousands publish their poems in one form or another but why are 500–1000 copies regarded as a respectable size for an edition of poems in Britain, when in other countries poetry books are produced in thousands and these editions sometimes run out within weeks? Is it easier for poets in these other countries to contribute to their societies' health and necessary medicine, because people take more notice of them? 'Blanking' is one of the most sophisticated weapons of the powers that rule Britain. We think, for example, of the hundreds of thousands of innocent people killed by 'the Allies' in the Gulf War; the news is not suppressed, merely rendered inactive. 'Blanking' is a formidable enemy of poetry in Britain today. Nevertheless poetry is alive. We would be in a much worse state if we were producing no poetry at all. Let Bunyan's Mr Great-Heart have the last word:

> This is like doing business in great Waters, or like going down into the deep; this is like being in the heart of the Sea, and like going down to the bottom of the Mountains; now it seems as if the Earth with its bars were about us for ever . . . For my part, as I have told you already, I have gone often through this Valley, and have been much harder put to it than now I am, and yet you see I am alive.

POETRY IN A DIFFERENT SOCIETY: NICARAGUA

By way of comparison we turn now to look at poetry in a very different society from ours: Central American, tropical, third-world Nicaragua, a tiny country with both an Atlantic and a Pacific coast.

In April 1954 the young poet Ernesto Cardenal took part in a failed conspiracy to overthrow his country's dictator Somoza. His friend Báez Bone was killed in the conspiracy and Ernesto, who had to go underground, wrote an epitaph for him:

> They thought they had buried
> you and what they did was bury a seed.[8]

Two years later in 1956 the poet Rigoberto López Pérez did succeed in killing Somoza. His last letter to his mother was cut up into lines and published as a poem by Carlos Fonseca.[9] (In his letter Rigoberto tells his mother he has taken out a life insurance policy for her in case he is killed – he was) :

> Although my comrades
> don't want to accept it
> I have decided to try to be
> the one
> who initiates
> the beginning of the end
> of this tyranny . . .
>
> I hope you will
> take all these things calmly
> and think what I have done
> is a duty any Nicaraguan
> who really
> loves their country
> should have performed
> a long time ago.

In 1961 Carlos Fonseca, Tomás Borge and Silvio Mayorga founded the Sandinista Front, to liberate their country still under the dictatorship of another Somoza. Carlos was killed fighting in 1976. Tomás describes how the news came to him in prison:[10]

> The governor of Tipitapa prison came gleefully to our small cell, with *Novedades* in his hand, to give us the news: Carlos Fonseca was dead. We were silent for a few moments and then replied: 'No Colonel, you are mistaken. Carlos Fonseca is one of the dead who never die.' The Colonel said to us: 'Really, you people are incredible.'

The poet and singer Carlos Mejía Godoy turned this incident into a famous song 'Comandante Carlos'.[11]

Tomás also wrote poetry in prison. Here is part of his 'Letter to Ana Josefina',[12] addressed to his little daughter on her second birthday:

> I don't known if I'll die
> when the cocks crow

this coming winter.
But if my hands grow cold
and my eyes lose
their teasing gleam
their tenderness
I shall live on.

I shall go on
if you are generous
if in your heart
egoism finds no room
and with your sweetness and your rage
you stand firm against injustices.

While he was in prison Tomás threatened his guards and torturers with revenge when the Sandinistas triumphed. His words were turned into a song by Carlos Mejía's brother Luis Enrique:[13]

My personal revenge will be your children's
right to schooling and to flowers . . .

My personal revenge will be to offer
these hands you once ill-treated
with all their tenderness intact.

After the Revolution Tomás became Minister of the Interior and got his revenge. He personally sought out his torturers and forgave them.

Tenderness is a constant theme in Sandinista poetry, which spills over into their revolutionary ideology. Another leader, Ricardo Morales who was killed at Nandaime in 1973 (together with Oscar Turcios), writes this love poem to his fellow militant and *compañera* Doris Tijerino (now a member of Parliament for Matagalpa). In Ricardo's poem[14] he and she are so close they are 'one life' and their tenderness for each other is indistinguishable from their common dedication to the Revolution. For him she is:

you who are mortal but
resist like the wind's resident backbone . . .

and the poem concludes:

> There is so much of your arms
> so much of your face
> so much of your tenderness
> as the substance of the universe
> and so much of my blood through your skin
> so much of your breath
> caught in my trembling
> and so much history
> and so much more
> that we are two forms
> and it is one life
> and everywhere there you are
> and the struggle continues.

Meanwhile in 1969 the twenty-year-old poet Leonel Rugama had decided to leave the seminary where he was training for the priesthood and join the Sandinista urban guerillas in Managua. He wrote a famous poem entitled 'The Earth is a Satellite of the Moon':[15]

> The Apollo 2 cost more than Apollo 1.
> Apollo 1 cost enough.
> Apollo 3 cost more than Apollo 2.
> Apollo 2 cost more than Apollo 1.
> Apollo 1 cost enough . . .
>
> The great grandparents of the Acahualinca people
> were less hungry than the grandparents.
> The great grandparents died of hunger.
> The grandparents of the Acahualinca people
> were less hungry than the fathers.
> The grandparents died of hunger . . .
> The children of the Acahualinca people
> are not born for hunger
> and they are hungry to be born
> in order to die of hunger.
> Blessed are the poor
> because theirs shall be the moon.

In his *Oracle concerning Managua*[16] Ernesto Cardenal gives a dramatic account of Leonel's heroic death defending a safe house in Managua against besieging troops, tanks and helicopters, and defying them to the last with most unpriestly insults. (The dictator made the mistake of televising the battle.) Later Cardenal's poem 'Final Offensive'[17] described the Sandinista victory with an acknowledgment to Leonel:

> It was like a trip to the moon
> with all its precise and complicated details . . .
>
> The moon was the earth. Our bit of earth.
> And we got there.
>   And now Rugama,
> it's beginning to belong to the poor; the earth is
> (with its moon).

Gioconda Belli describes Nicaragua as a heroic fighter:[18]

> . . . the girl who sways her body provokes
> winks sells *tamales* sells paintings
> does her bit in the militia
> goes to the park invents love
> sets the flame trees alight
> flirts playing hide and seek
> walks out among fixed bayonets
> makes circus makes holiday prays
> and believes in living and dying
> brandishes her fiery sword
> to ensure the only choice for anyone
> is heaven on earth
> or ashes
> a free country
> or death.

Quite a lot of the Sandinista guerillas were women. The poet Daisy Zamora[19] ran the clandestine Radio Sandino and describes her encounter with Ernesto Cardenal:

> If I had known Ernesto as he appears
> in a yellowing photo Julio showed me,
> thin, bearded, check shirt, linen trousers,
> hands in his pockets

and a general air of helplessness,
I would have joined the April Rebellion for him . . .

After the 78 insurrection
at last he came to me.
He appeared in the clandestine Radio Sandino
wanting to meet me because he had heard
I was a poet and combatant . . .
He arrived quietly, with no fuss
walking through the rainy mountain.
He came into the booth and asked for me.

After the Revolution Ernesto became Minister of Culture and Daisy
Vice-Minister. After becoming a catholic priest in 1965 Cardenal
had established a peasant community on Solentiname, a group of
islands on Lake Nicaragua. Here the first poetry workshop was
set up in 1976. The peasants, some previously illiterate, produced
some remarkable poems. They became increasingly involved with
the Sandinistas and all the young men and women in the poetry
workshop took part in the Assault on San Carlos in October 1977.
In a characteristic oxymoron Carlos Mejía's song about the assault
describes them as 'armed to the teeth with tenderness'. Felipe Peña,
killed in May 1979, addresses a disgruntled girlfriend:[20]

You think I am not in love
and you think I am a sod
because I act as if I don't get
the meaning of your words
your tone of voice, your wicked looks.
Possibly you doubt your beauty
because I don't seem to make much of it.
I don't want you to think of me like that.
Please reflect. Consider
what can a guerilla offer you
squelching in mud
along mountain paths . . .

When Ernesto Cardenal became Minister of Culture in 1979, the
Solentiname workshop became the model for the poetry workshops
he set up all over the country: in small towns, army barracks, police
stations . . . He issued some guidelines for writing poems which

begin: 'Writing good poetry is easy and the rules for doing it are few and simple.' The guidelines caution against thumping rhymes and metres; they recommend the use of particular rather than general terms: 'iguana' rather than just 'animal', 'flame-tree' rather than just 'tree'. 'Poetry has an added appeal if it includes proper names' of people, rivers, towns etc. Rather than being based on ideas poetry should be based on things which reach us through our senses. We should write as we speak with the natural plainness of the spoken language, not the written language. Avoid clichés or hackneyed expressions. Try to condense the language as much as possible; all words which are not absolutely necessary should be left out. Cardenal's name for the kind of poetry he is recommending is 'exteriorist'.

Although we may smile at this exotic bossiness, much of it is excellent advice, particularly for new writers of poetry who may think it is 'poetic' to use flowery archaic cliché and circumlocution. We may also recall that the extract from Blake's *Jerusalem* quoted earlier is an excellent example of 'poetry having added appeal if it includes proper names'. In Chapter 4 we noted that Wordsworth argued strongly against a special 'poetic' diction, Hopkins said the language of poetry should not be obsolete, Sassoon dismissed some of his own earlier work as 'too noble' and Eliot said 'poetry must not stray too far from the ordinary everyday language we use and hear.' This is what Tom Paulin, in his collection of essays, *Minotaur, Poetry and the Nation State*[21], calls 'orality'.

Within eight months of the Sandinista triumph a massive literacy campaign was mounted (run by Ernesto's brother Fernando Cardenal), which reduced illiteracy from over 50% to under 13% and won a UNESCO prize. Poetry was an important part of the campaign. The literacy teachers, mainly young student volunteers, known as *brigadistas*, wrote many poems (subsequently published in an anthology by the Ministry of Culture) and used poetry in their teaching. The Ministry published a poetry magazine *Poesía Libre* (edited by the poet Julio Valle-Castillo), containing poems by well known Nicaraguans, translations from many countries and a regular section of Nicaraguan workshop poetry. These magazines were on sale cheaply in supermarkets and many other outlets. During the 1980s the Editorial Nueva Nicaragua published many books of poetry regularly in editions of 6000 and often much larger. (Gioconda's Belli's poem quoted above comes from *De la costilla de Eva* published in 1987 in an edition of 15,000. Nicaraguan books usually have the edition size printed on them. Perhaps British poetry publishers would not dare!) This was in a country with a population of three million, over half of whom had been illiterate before 1979. The Ministry of Culture also ran an annual Poetry Marathon in the amphitheatre in the garden of their national poet Ruben Darío's house. In 1988 (when this author took part) it was presided over by President Daniel Ortega (also a poet) and Ernesto Cardenal. Daisy Zamora and many other well known Nicaraguan poets read poems, as did anyone else who wanted to.

The prominence given to poetry had important effects on the Nicaraguan revolution. Like the land, the culture, both past and present was 'redistributed' to its rightful owners, the people. And as with the land, those who possess it, can both produce and enjoy its bounty. People not only learnt to read in order to 'consume' poetry but also produced it in large quantities. Obviously the quality varied considerably. But even producers of very ordinary little poems benefited from an enormous growth in self-respect through this act of 'speaking for themselves'. As the seven-year-old Solentiname poet Juan Agudelo[22] puts it:

> I am happy because I have my parents.
> I am happy because I can read.
> I am happy because I am a poet.

Another important role for poetry was its epic function in telling the story of the Revolution with its heroes and martyrs again and again so that it became part of the fabric of the Nicaraguan mind. This example and encouragement was no small factor in enabling them to withstand for eleven years the force and horror of US determination to destroy their revolution. The brothers Carlos and Luis Enrique Mejía Godoy wrote the *Canto Epico to the FSLN*,[23] a song cycle telling the whole story of the revolution in songs, first sung and broadcast clandestinely, later well known by all. When Sandinista heroes are buried, their names are read out and all the people respond: '¡Presente!', as to a roll call. Meaning the dead are still present as long as their memory and the Revolution they died for still lives. The chorus verse of Carlos Mejía's song 'Comandante Carlos' ends: 'All Nicaragua proclaims you: ¡Presente!' And here indeed the words are not merely referential but performative: the act of singing the song *keeps* the hero present. Julio Valle-Castillo has written a set of poems amounting to a

Sandinista martyrology[24] and can also amuse his readers, as in the poem comparing a baby nephew's progress to the revolution's:

> No sooner born than he shouts and screams
> clenching his fists like little contact bombs.
> For the Final Offensive he became expert
> at shooting under beds with his mother,
> retreating to Doña Ermida's breast –
> a granny at last – or nights beneath
> rockets and mortar shells.
> Fat and ugly the awful child,
> pretty as a Sherman tank
> just captured from the Guard,
> advanced snatching sunlit days from death.
>
> The Revolution and he began to look better,
> handsome the pair of them,
> but my nephew got a nasty bout of measles.
> Let's hope the Revolution won't catch anything . . .
> We are besotted with her,
> giving her all her medicines at the right time.

Part of the pleasure of the poem lies in enjoying the allusion to the famous tactical *retreat* to Masaya in June 1979 ordered by the Sandinistas, three weeks before their *advance* to enter Managua in triumph on 19 July.

The extracts from poems quoted above are a very small sample of work from a population not much more than one third that of London, where so many of those involved in the Revolution wrote poetry, knew each other, fell in love with each other, wrote poetry about each other, all contributing to a tightly interwoven sense of belonging to a country which, though little and poor, was exceedingly rich in poetry. A surprising amount of the poetry is in fact love poetry, although Nicaraguans would find the suspicion of political poetry felt by certain literary circles in England extraordinary. As Daniel Ortega puts it (in a poem written in prison in the 1960s):[25]

> Moon! Lilies! God,
> these a-political poets!

This poem, which gives a very strong sense of the dislocation and near-madness induced by long imprisonment and torture, ends laconically:

> We missed Managua
> in mini skirts.

Ortega became president, the novelist Sergio Ramirez vice-president, Ernesto Cardenal Minister of Culture, Daisy Zamora Vice-Minister of Culture and Tomás Borge Minister of the Interior. Many others in the government or high positions after the Revolution were also poets. The third important effect of poetry on Nicaraguan society was that the poets' ideas actually shaped Nicaraguan revolutionary thought and policy: poets became *acknowledged legislators*. For many years Cardenal had had the same role as the *chilan*, the wise priest-poet-seer he wrote about in his *Homage to the American Indians*. Cardenal's poems had not only denounced the evils of the dictatorship but imagined in detail what a good society would be like and what sort of spirit it should have. (In Chapter 4 we quoted his poem describing what, for him is 'putting your finger on communism *compañeros*'.) Now here is Cardenal describing a meeting of the new poet-filled cabinet:[26]

> We are summoned to a cabinet meeting
> knowing in advance it is for a very serious reason
> but not what.
> All the ministers and directors of self-governing bodies
> round the big table.
> And it was a serious reason:
> the setting up of an Emergency National Committee
> to deal with the danger of a plague of *Aedes Aegypti*
>   mosquitoes . . .
>
> Small and dark
> they carry an infection
> with a high mortality rate among children
> and dangerous to the old.
> Very possibly there will be an outbreak in Nicaragua . . .
>
> I look at the serious faces round the big table
> strewn with files, ashtrays,

and I think: how odd,
how very odd. It is love.
The cabinet meeting for love of their neighbour.

Or here is his 'Economic Report':[27]

I am surprised to find myself reading
with great interest
things like
cotton harvest twenty five percent up
on last year
coffee exports US$124.2 million . . .

When did such data ever interest me before?
It is because now our wealth
however little
is to be
for everyone.
So it is
for the people,
love of the people,
this interest.
Love is now the meaning of these figures . . .

Soft cloud-whirl cotton
– we went singing to the cotton-cutting,
in our fingers we held clouds –
will become roads, zinc roofs,
the economic has become poetic
or rather, with the Revolution
economics now is love.

As Shelley said in his *Defence of Poetry*:

The most unfailing herald, companion and follower of the
awakening of a great people to work a beneficial change in
opinion or institution is Poetry. At such periods there is an accu-
mulation of the power of communicating and receiving intense
and impassioned conceptions respecting man and nature.

Poetry is language in power, world-creating word. 'The Revolution
is the imagination in power' to transform an unjust world. The

threat of this good example was the cause of President Reagan's hysterical hatred. Like the devil, the US government assumes the right to be 'prince of this world' and for Nicaragua this prince was indeed Doctor of Death and the power of darkness. Whatever the successes and failures of the Nicaraguan Revolution, poetry was involved at every level in what it attempted and – despite an election setback in 1990 which must have caused a disappointment as bitter as Milton's – has not lost hope of achieving.

In a speech[28] made in Spain in 1990 after the election defeat, Tomás Borge says that despite his country's dire poverty and distress, he believes they have something of great value to offer us, a gift for 1992. He addresses the people of Europe and his words particularly concern poets. So to end this chapter on poetry in society here is a view of us from the outside, which is both a castigation and an invitation:

Although Europeans retain their cultural heritage, they prefer for the most part the expensive and dehumanising trinkets of consumerist society. Citizens of the old continent, I invite you to step out of your gloom. You have conquered everything and all you have gained is individual isolation. Now it is your turn to discover for yourselves a sense of community with all human kind . . .

Contemporary Latin American philosophy, also called for obvious reasons the philosophy of liberation, is concerned with an integrative and kindly humanism which considers the liberation of humanity as the basic objective of culture. . . . This is the finest utopia ever conceived in the history of Latin America: the new human being. Creating this new human being for the citizens of the twenty-first century will be our most valuable contribution to humanity . . .

We will never treat anyone like an animal – which is what the colonists called our ancestors. We will treat all like human beings. The day when all people treat each other as equals will be the day when revolution will have been perfected in this savage and contradictory world . . . The new human beings we have discovered in Latin America will conquer Europe, not in order to colonise it but in order to liberate it, so that its own mythical ceremonies can be initiated afresh and rise again from their solemn and wonderful burial ground . . . [for] the liberty and enjoyment of all the peoples of the earth.

NOTES

1. In John Heath-Stubbs, *Collected Poems*.
2. *Ephesians* 4:8.
3. Part of this poem was used as example I at the end of Chapters 1 and 2. It is published in *Witness to Magic*.
4. Christopher Hampton, *The Ideology of the Text* (Buckingham: Open University Press, 1990).
5. *Revelation* 22:1–2.
6. Richard Holmes' *Coleridge Early Visions* (London: Penguin, 1989) is a fascinating biography. See also Stevie Smith's 'Thoughts about the Person from Porlock', quoted in Chapter 4.
7. Anne Acland, *A Devon Family. The Story of the Aclands* (Chichester: Phillimore and Co., 1981).
8. 'Epitafio para la tumba de Adolfo Báez Bone' by Ernesto Cardenal in *Poesía Política Nicaragüense*, ed. Francisco de Asis Fernández (Managua: Ministry of Culture, 1986). This poem and many of the other Nicaragaun poems quoted in this chapter appear in *Nicaragua: Poetry and Revolution (1954–90)*, a bi-lingual anthology of Nicaraguan poetry to be published by Katabasis, London.
9. From 'Carta-Testamento' by Rigoberto López-Pérez in *Poesía Política Nicaragüense*.
10. From 'Carlos el amanecer ya no es una tentación' by Tomás Borge in *Nicaráuac 13* (Managua 1986). Translation of the whole text appears in *Carlos Fonseca* by Tomás Borge *et. al.* to be published by Katabasis.
11. The song 'Comandante Carlos' is on the cassette *Guitarra Armada* distributed in Britain by the Nicaragua Solidarity Campaign (NSC), Red Rose Club, 129 Seven Sisters Road, London N7. Text and translation appear in *Carlos Fonseca*.
12. 'Carta a Ana Josefina' by Tomás Borge is in *La ceremonía esperada* (Managua: Editorial Nueva Nicaragua, 1990). Translation is by D. L.
13. Song 'Mi Venganza Personal' by Luis Enrique Mejía Godoy is on the cassette *Yo soy de un pueblo sencillo* (from NSC). Translation is in *Keeping Heart*.
14. From 'Me es necesario tu cuerpo' in Ricardo Morales Avilés, *Obras* (Managua: Editorial Nueva Nicaragua, 1981). Translation 'Your Body is Necessary to Me' by D. L. is in *In the Shadow of Columbus* (Leicester: Leicester-Masaya Link Group, 1992).
15. Title poem in *La Tierra es un satélite de la luna* by Leonel Rugama, (Managua: Editorial Nueva Nicaragua, 1985).
16. Originally published in 1973. Translation by Robert Pring-Mill in *Zero Hour and Other Documentary Poems* (New York: New

Directions, 1980).

17. 'Ofensiva Final' by Ernesto Cardenal in *Vuelos de Victoria* (León University: León, Nicaragua 1985). Translation in *Nicaraguan New Time*

18. 'Nicaragua agua fuego' by Gioconda Belli in *De la costilla de Eva* (Managua: Editorial Nueva Nicaragua, 1986). This translation is by D. L. For another translation see Chapter 6.

19. '50 versos de amor y una confesión no realizada a Ernesto Cardenal' by Daisy Zamora in *En limpio se escribe la vida* (Managua: Editorial Nueva Nicaragua, 1988).

20. 'Vos creés' by Felipe Peña in *Poesía campesina de Solentiname* (Managua: Ministry of Culture, 1980). This translation by D. L. Other poems by this community are in *The Peasant Poets of Solentiname*, bi-lingual text translated by Peter Wright (London: Katabasis, 1990).

21. Tom Paulin, *Minotaur. Poetry and the Nation State* (London: Faber and Faber, 1992).

22. In *The Peasant Poets of Solentiname*.

23. The *Canto Epico al FSLN* is available on cassette from NSC. A bi-lingual text translated by D. L. is published in *The Nicaraguan Epic* (London: Katabasis, 1989).

24. *Materia Jubilosa* by Julio Valle-Castillo (Managua: Editorial Nueva Nicaragua, 1986). Some of these poems, collected under the title *Nicaraguan Vision and Other Poems* are published in bi-lingual text in *The Nicaraguan Epic*.

25. 'En la prisión' by Daniel Ortega in *Poesía Política Nicaragüense*.

26. 'Reunión de Gabinete' by Ernesto Cardenal in *Vuelos de Victoria*.

27. 'Economic Report' is translated from the poet's typescript in *Nicaraguan New Time*.

28. Quoted in *1992 and the New World* (Leicester: Leicester-Masaya Link Group, 1991).

6

Translating Poetry

Coleridge says that what makes a poem is its

> untranslatableness in words of the same language without injury
> to the meaning. Be it observed that I include in the meaning of
> a word not only its correspondent object but likewise all the
> associations which it recalls.

Not only must each word in a poem be selected with such economy
and precision that no other word will do. But a good poem has all
the particularity of a recognisable individual voice. It is word made
flesh. If poetry is untranslatable in words of the same language,
it must surely be even more difficult to translate poetry from
another language expressing a different culture and society. Here
the speaker-poet is not only a different individual body but also
belongs to a different social body or body politic. 'Poetry is what
is lost in translation.' However, it could be argued there is no need
to translate poetry in words of the same language because speakers
of that language have access to it. We do not have access to poetry in
languages we cannot understand so there is a need for translation.

We said the poet should avoid archaic language. A translation
of a poem is likely to have more power if it is translated into
the language the translator speaks in her own *time* and *place*. This
means that there can be countless translations into the language of
different times and places. Translations into US English often fail to
move speakers of English English and sometimes make them cringe.
Likewise US English speakers may dislike a translation that sounds
'too British'. A translation made in the nineteenth century requires a
double effort from the reader: to try and grasp the place and time of
the original and the place and time of the translator in a society very
different from today. Nevertheless if a translator tries to give energy
to the translation by using very 'up to the minute' language and a
lot of contemporary 'in-words' this work may date very quickly.

This chapter does not attempt a theory of translation. It looks at the special problems of poetry translation in relation to the idea of poetry as a particular body of language operating in a particular time and place. It proceeds by inviting the reader to look closely at, and sometimes compare, various examples of poetry translation. In all the examples below the reader is invited to read the translation *out loud* and if possible the original when given (with pronunciation help from someone who speaks the language, if necessary). Secondly, please note that inevitably it has not always been possible to quote whole poems and the parts of poems extracted cannot show the poem's full shape. Thirdly, particularly when various translations of the same text are juxtaposed, comment is often confined to a particular feature of a translation. This allows readers to do most of the work of comparison and draw their own conclusions. When an original text is quoted followed by a literal 'crib' and then by a translator's final version, the reader might like to have a go at making the literal crib into a poem – or part of a poem – in English before looking at what the quoted translator has done. It can be fun to do this in a group and compare your efforts. Discussing different translations of the same poem can also be an enjoyable exercise for a group, so the extracts here can be used to try this out.

THREE KINDS OF POETRY TRANSLATION

Traditionally (after Dryden) a distinction has been made between three ways of translating poetry: metaphrase (a literal translation or crib), imitation (a completely free version or variation which transposes the text in any way it wants) and the middle way, to which Dryden gives the rather unsatisfactory name of paraphrase ('translation with some latitude'). All these types of translation may be valuable and have different uses. At the two extremes, the literal translation or crib on the one hand and the completely free 'imitation' on the other do not have to tackle the problem of voice that challenges the middle way, which is what we normally think of as poetry translation. The literal translation or crib does not even attempt to sound like an English poem and the completely free version or 'imitation' is not concerned with retaining the voice of the original.

Literal Translation or Crib

The literal translation or 'crib', Dryden's 'metaphrase', is very useful for example in small print as a footnote to the Penguin Lorca and the Penguin Rimbaud printed in the original Spanish and French respectively. With the crib and a smattering of the language concerned or even other Latin languages, the reader can gain considerable enjoyment from hearing and reading these foreign poems.

The Completely Free Version or Imitation

A recent, perhaps extreme, example of 'imitation' is Walcott's *Omeros*,[1] a huge poem transposing Homer's epic theme into Caribbean culture and not at all bound to Homer's text. This could be described as a form of allusion rather than translation.

'All I have against translation is that it can't be done!' says Nicholas Moore. He goes on to produce more than thirty English versions or 'imitations' of Baudelaire's poem 'Spleen',[2] which begins:

> Je suis comme le roi d'un pays pluvieux
> Riche, mais impuissant, jeune et pourtant très-vieux.

Literally this means 'I am like the king of a rainy country, rich but powerless/impotent, young but all too old.' Moore transposes Baudelaire's poem into many different voices and contexts. The task was undertaken for fun and many of the the versions are strictly parody, often highly entertaining. Although these voices are not Moore's, the whole enterprise of transposing Baudelaire's *maudit* Parisian gloom to Cambridge wit expresses the translator. Here are some examples:

1.   I am like the Dave-Ap-Gwilym of a wet English county,
      Well-greased but gormless, ancient but randy . . .

2.   I am the T. S. Eliot of new wastelands;
      Fertile, but powerless; young but with tied hands . . .

3.   I am like the laird of many rainy acres,
      A rich man, but gey powerless, young, but jaded,

Distrustful of advisers and smooth talkers,
Whose joy in dogs and coursing too has faded . . .

4.   I'm like the Führer of some Southern State,
        Too young for President, too old for mate,
        Sick of the intellectuals, whose advice
        Is dog-gone nigger-talk, all peas and rice . . .

Cicely Herbert made a punk song version called 'I'm Pissed Off'! It
begins:

The world is a cigarette and life is a drag.

Now look at another example of a version or 'imitation' of a very
different text. Here is part of Psalm 58 in the Revised Standard
version of the Bible [1] (itself a translation, of course). It is set beside
a translation of Ernesto Cardenal's version [2], which transposes the
psalm into the modern world:[3]

1. *RSV*:

    Do you indeed decree what is right, you gods?
    Do you judge the sons of men uprightly?
    Nay, in your hearts you devise wrongs;
    your hands deal out violence on earth.

2. *Cardenal*:

    You defenders of Law and Order
    isn't your law on the side of one class?
    Civil Law to protect private property
    Penal Law to harass the oppressed
    The freedom you speak of is freedom for capital
    your 'free world' is free exploitation . . .

1. *RSV*:

    The righteous will rejoice when he sees the vengeance;
    he will bathe his feet in the blood of the wicked.

Men will say, 'Surely there is a reward for the righteous; surely there is a God who judges on earth.'

2. *Cardenal*:

The people shall enjoy themselves in the exclusive clubs
they will take possession of private firms . . .
In great city squares we shall celebrate
the anniversary of the Revolution.
The God who exists is of the proletariat.

The Middle Way: Translation with 'Some Latitude'

The middle way, translation 'with some latitude' (Dryden uses the term 'paraphrase' in a rather different sense from the modern one), is probably what most people think of as a poem translation. The translator tries to make the translation a poem in English, conveying as much as possible of the original's meaning and feeling.

VOICE

The translator has to make decisions about the voice in which the translated poem speaks. As we noted above, the problem of voice does not arise with a literal crib on the one hand or a completely free version on the other. But with the middle way it is a major factor in the quality of the translation. If the translator is also a poet and tries to make the translation a good poem in English, it will inevitably have some of the translator's tones of voice. Or may even sound like an original poem by the translator. The Irish poet Nuala Ní Dhomhnaill also writes in English but her book *Pharaoh's Daughter*[4] sets her original Irish beside translations by different famous Irish poets, Seamus Heaney, Eilean Ní Chuilleanain, and others. Many of the translations are beautiful poems in English and it is interesting to hear how strongly some of these well-known poets have produced translations that sound just like their own poems. However, this is a special case because poet and most of the translators are native speakers of both Irish and English and to some extent share a common culture.

When, as is usually the case, poet and translator do not have the same mother tongue or share the same culture, new problems arise. On the one hand a translator who is poet enough to make the translation a good poem cannot betray his or her own voice. But the hearer of the translation wants to hear not only a good poem in English but in some way also the voice of the original poet. You cannot just make an English poem that the writer of the original might have produced if she had been a native English speaker. If the writer of the original had been a native English speaker she or he would probably not have written that poem because a poem in a different language is normally the product of a different culture. But a too literal translation may sound like a foreigner speaking English, even a form of pidgin, which devalues the poem. A translation could be compared to a baby, with two parents, and perhaps resembling one parent more than the other. At the end of *Middlemarch* Mrs Vincy is consoled for the disappointment of her darling son Fred's marriage to plain Mary Garth, by her grandchildren: 'at least two of Fred's boys were real Vincys and did not *feature the Garths'*. But proud grandmothers can be unhelpful, especially to a daughter-in-law considered not good enough.

POETRY AS INCARNATE WORD

A voice belongs to a body. From the beginning this book has stressed the need for poetry to be *incarnate, embodied, rooted* in the particular. Not only are poet and translator different individual bodies probably belonging to different social bodies, countries perhaps, the poem is also a body of language. Some translations do not seem to have a substantial body of their own and sound like a ghost of the original. Being translated can be an eerie experience for the poet and if the poet dislikes the translation (but needs it, as in the case of exiles), he may feel nightmarishly like a ghost failing to get back into a transformed body it cannot inhabit. For now the body is dead or possessed by an alien spirit. The problem of poetry translation is that both the original poem and the translation should be incarnate word, incarnate in different material conditions, but in some sense the *same* word.[5]

The chorus of one of the great popular songs of liberation theology goes:[6]

Cristo ya nació
en Palacagüina

del Chepe Pavón
y una tal Maria.
Ella va planchar
muy humildemente
la ropa que cosa
la mujer hermosa
del terrateniente.

Literally this means: Now Christ is born in Palacagüina from Chepe
Pavón and any Maria. She is going to iron very humbly the dress
that (is sewing) the beautiful wife of the landowner (i.e. the dress
the landowner's beautiful wife is sewing) Palacagüina is a small
poor Nicaraguan village, the village carpenter is called 'Chepe', a
familiar form of José, just as in English Jo is short for Joseph. This
carpenter is known as 'el (the) Chepe', as in Yorkshire he might be
'our Jo'. As in many catholic countries, all the girls in the village are
called Maria and the child's mother could be any of them. Maria is
then situated in her social class: a low one; she is a domestic servant.
In the song the Indian neighbours bring presents for her baby. When
her husband Chepe is getting rheumatism Maria hopes her son will
grow up to help him in his carpentry work. But 'el cipote piensa,
"Mañana quiero ser guerrillero"': 'The lad thinks: "One day I want to
be a guerilla". To join the liberation struggle, in which the crucified
people rise . . . Here liberation theology is making the same point
about Christ (the incarnate word) as we have been making about
poetry (also incarnate word): it is the *particularity* of its setting that
makes it effective and gives it its saving grace. Hence the difficulty
of translation.

Now look at the task of translating the chorus of the song. We
have the option of 'imitation' and transferring the whole context to,
say, Yorkshire during the miners' strike – particular to particular.
This might produce a good song but because it would be embodied
in a completely different context, its relation to the original would
be tenuous. On the other hand the above 'metaphrase' translation
conveys very little of the original's power, arising from the particularity, the incarnate quality of the *actual original words and music in
their original context*. We who are outside that culture can only feel
the song's force indirectly, once we have acquired a certain amount
of cultural and linguistic information (e.g. the status of 'el Chepe'
and 'una tal Maria'), information which actually *shapes* the people
to whom this culture belongs and makes them what they are: it is

internal to them but external to us, or rather we are external to it. So that is our first problem. Even a 'middle way' translation will only communicate to those initiated by imaginative sympathy.

Our next problem is a more strictly linguistic one. In the first quatrain it is extremely difficult not only to reproduce the compelling rhythm but also to convey all the original nuances. If we translate:

> So now Christ is born
> in Palacagüina
> from our Chepe Pavón
> and this or that Maria

this is an improvement rhythmically on the previous 'crib' translation, but a good deal else is still lacking. I cannot think of any English phrase to convey the full quality of 'una tal Maria' in this context. In the second part, the last five lines, of the chorus we have not only a new rhythmic challenge but a rhyme scheme that is almost a tongue twister. (Try saying the Spanish fast: the tune is fast.) Having illustrated the almost insuperable difficulties, at this point I leave the reader with the challenge.

TRANSLATION DIFFICULTIES AND CHALLENGES

Metre

A well known problem with translating songs or verse that is in metre from one language to another is that some languages tend to take longer to say some things than others. For example, Spanish often takes longer to say something than English. So if you are keeping to a metre, especially if the translation is intended for singing, the English may feel tempted to 'pad' (generally not good for poetry) or, in order to avoid this, find itself introducing extra ideas. For example, four lines from the 'Gloria' of the *Misa Campesina*:[7]

1	con el gozo desbordante
2	y explosivo de los cohetes
3	que iluminan nuestros cielos
4	en la fiesta popular.

Originally this was translated:

1   with joy overflowing
2   and bursting like the rockets
3   that light up our skies
4   on a festival night.

This has already introduced the 'extra' word night. But it was still too succinct to be sung to the music. For the English to fit the music the third line had to expand to:

that light up our skies with colour

This gives line 3 eight syllables in Spanish (in singing que-i are elided into one syllable) and eight syllables in English. Line 4 has seven syllables in Spanish and six in English, so the singers had to make 'val', the last syllable of 'festival' into two syllables:

on a fest-i-və-l night.

As the Spanish syllables have almost equal weight, the English equivalent still sounded slightly distorted because it comes naturally to us to 'swallow' some syllables and stress others.

As we noted in Chapter 1, this distortion of the natural rhythm of spoken English may also occur in English songs that are not a translation. Milton is a poet with an excellent ear and his hymn 'Let us with a gladsome mind' fits the alternating beat/offbeat tune well. But when we sing:

Lét us/ wíth a/gládsome/ mínd

we put an unnatural stress on 'with'.

When a translation is not meant for singing the translator must decide how closely to keep the form of the original. Sometimes a translation which sticks religiously to the metre and rhyme scheme of the original may appear dead or forced in English. See below under 'Translations of Rilke' for an example of this.

Sound

The dictionary equivalents of words in my language may have completely different sounds and rhythm from words in the original language. The translator must try to find words that not only convey a dictionary meaning but the feeling of the original poem.

We have already noted that only English cocks crow 'cock-a-doodle-doo'. What we might call 'semantic onomatopoeia' presents another, sometimes insuperable, problem to the translator. To stick to bird-language, for example, in a short poem by the five-year-old poet Irene Agudelo[8], very early in the morning she hears a cockatoo saying:

> Quiero mangos maduros
> quiero mangos maduros.

This means 'I want ripe mangos'. But in spite of one word being the same, this does not reproduce the *sound* of what the cockatoo says in Spanish and in translation the poem loses a great deal of its charm. A more successful translation of bird language comes in Peter Wright's translation of another poem from the peasant poets of Solentiname, this time by Pedro Pablo Meneses. In Spanish the nightjars sing happily: 'Jodido, rejodido', which Wright renders as 'Screw you, I'll do you'.[9]

Sometimes we are able to reproduce or reconstitute poetic devices in the original by what seems a happy accident. For example the alliteration in Augustine's phrase 'colligens totum quod sum a dispersione et deformitate hac'[10] reappears rather neatly in the translation: 'gathering all that I am from this muddle and mess', a far more vigorous rendering than keeping 'dispersion' and 'deformity' in English would have been.

When Groddeck's Soul-Seeker announces 'pissend ist wissend' this can be reproduced neatly as 'peeing is seeing'.

Word Order

It is sometimes better to alter the word order of the original for the sound, rhythm or some other reason. In Chapter 2 we quoted the penultimate line of Ernesto Cardenal's poem 'The US Congress Approves Contra Aid'. We gave the (phonic) reasons why the order of a list of things pillaged by the Contra in an attack had been changed from the literal: 'The coffee beans, their small animals, their small houses, everything' to 'The coffee beans, cottages, animals everything'. Likewise the poem 'New Ecology'[11] ends in Spanish:

La liberación no soló la ansiaban los humanos.
Toda la ecología gemía. La revolución
es tambíen de lagos, ríos, árboles, animales.

The literal order of the list in the last line is: lakes, rivers, trees,
animals. In the English translation below, the previous paragraph of
the poem ends with the word 'kiskadees' but this rhyme with 'trees'
(seven lines up so it does not thump!) was not the main reason for
changing the order of the last line:

Not only humans longed for liberation.
All ecology groaned. The revolution
is also for animals, rivers, lakes and trees.

Here, as in the 'Contra Aid' poem, the vowel *order* makes the list
sound more cumulative. The word 'also' contains the only back
vowels and introduces the four items in the list which, apart from
schwa, have all front vowels in order from open to close: /ɪz
ɔ:lsəʊ fər ænɪmɔlz rɪvɔz leɪkz ən tri:z/. With this modification
of the list in the English translation, the rhythm also supports
the meaning better. The stresses come closer together at the end
of the line:

. . . álsŏ fŏr/ ánĭmǎls/ rívĕrs/ lákes ănd/ trées/

This rhythm is reinforced by the zero-consonant alliteration of the
initial two dactyls: 'also for animals'. The closing vowel order is
reinforced by the fact that the vowels in the monosyllabic two final
words in the list are long: /eɪ/ and /i:/, whereas the vowels in
the words 'animals' and 'rivers' are all short. Rhythm and sound
work together. Note however, that before changing the word order
of a list for reasons of sound and rhythm, the translator should
also consider whether the original order is important for others
reasons.

One more example of slight changes in the last line of a poem
to give it a better sound and body in English is in the previously
quoted poem 'Meditation in a DC-3'. The translation has a bit of
a pun in English, which seems legitimate as it is faithful to the
original's intentions. The poem ends with a list of various kinds
of human touching leading up to the conclusion, which reads in
the original:

es como tocar el comunismo con el dedo compañeros.

Literally translated this reads:

is like touching communism with the finger *compañeros*

In the final translation this changed to:

human touching human,
human skin meeting human skin
is putting your finger on communism *compañeros*.

Puns and Anagrams

Puns and punning anagrams can obviously be a problem. For example in his *Cosmic Canticle* Ernesto Cardenal plays with the similarity between ADAN (= the Spanish name for Adam, the first man) and ADN (Spanish anagram for DNA, i.e the life molecule), in a way that cannot be done in English. It would be difficult to translate the advertisement when our water was sold: 'BE AN H_2 OWNER' into another language.

Some puns are bi-lingual. For example a baker's near Farringdon Station is called 'Le Pain D'Amour'. To appreciate this pun an English speaker needs to know that 'le pain' means 'bread' in French and also to know that 'Chagrin d'amour' in the song means 'the pain of love'. French speakers would miss the pun altogether unless they knew the English meaning of 'pain'.

Humour

Humour often does not translate. Local place names may have strong associations in a particular culture. I think it would be hard to convey in any other language why all his audience burst out laughing when a bitterly disappointed lover began a poem addressed to the woman who had betrayed him:

No more balmy nights in Hampstead!

We saw in Ernesto Cardenal's 'Guidelines' that he recommended the use of particular names. When these have strong associations, partly humorous, these may be very obscure to the reader of a translation who belongs to another culture. For example in the lines:[12]

> Across the canal adolescent
> willows reserve the wildlife
> where Ken introduced newts

every Londoner knows that this is Ken Livingstone leader of the GLC when it supported many projects such as this Wildlife Reserve, and also that his newt-fancying caused much amusement. A Parisian might think Ken was just any English boy. Proper names are part of the particularity and humour of the incarnate word which make it virtually impossible that it should be 'the same' in another language.

IMAGES, SYMBOLS, ASSOCIATIONS

Different societies may express their feelings with different images and symbols and the translator has the task of deciding how much of the culture to translate.

Weather and Seasons

Most cultures use weather and seasons as symbols. 'April is the cruellest month' means something quite different in a tropical society which has no spring and only two seasons, one hot and dry and the other hot and wet. English people who long for a fine summer day have to use considerable imagination to feel the desolation in John of the Cross saying 'my soul is dry'. Some inland plains in Spain suffer punishing dusty heat with no rain for months on end.

Plants

Flowers and fruits are other common symbols which may give the translator problems. A Romanian love poem says of a woman 'she is a black pomegranate'. The English translator kept this image, whereas a US translator felt it was unintelligible and changed it to 'she is a ripe peach', which gives a completely different ('Florida') effect. In Carlos Mejía's song for Carlos Fonseca mentioned in the

Chapter 5, when Fonseca is shot dead in Zinica forest: 'trinitaria roja tu pecho desnudo'. 'Trinitaria' is heartsease, the viola or wild pansy (considerably bigger in the tropics). This flower has a black spot in the middle like a bullet and splaying purple petals like the blood. So in English we can translate: 'On your bare breast heartsease flowered' and feel something of the original solemnity . But if we say 'your naked breast was a wild pansy' our listeners will just laugh. It appears that the German for heartsease is 'Stiefmütterchen': 'little stepmother', which would make complete nonsense, giving the German translator an even worse headache than the English. The 'folk' name 'heartsease' worked best in the above example, perhaps by a happy accident. When the folk name conveys some obviously recognisable quality of the plant, it is likely to work better than the technical name. For example 'golden trumpet tree' is usually a better translation of 'cortés' (a tree with bright yellow trumpet shaped flowers) than 'tabebuia cyrsantha' and 'flame tree' (or 'flamboyant') is usually better than 'poinciana' for the tree with brilliant scarlet flowers called 'malinche' in Nicaragua. However, other considerations may occur.

Here are two versions of a few lines from the poem 'Nicaragua Water Fire'[13] by Gioconda Belli, quoted in Chapter 5:

1.   envy of the girl who sways her hips who struts around
       winks her eye sells *tamales* sells paintings
       serves in the militia goes to the park invents love
       ignites the *malinche* tree . . .

2.   envying the girl who sways her body provokes
       winks sells *tamales* sells paintings
       does her bit in the militia
       goes to the park invents love
       sets the flame trees alight . . .

Translation 1 keeps the original exotic-sounding Nicaraguan tree name 'malinche'. Translation 2 translates it as 'flame tree'. The reader has to decide whether you prefer to hear the (perhaps unintelligible) resonance of the original tree name or whether the translated English name 'flame tree' works on the poetic as well as the botanical level. In Central American tradition 'Malinche' was also the name of a famous, or rather infamous, Indian princess who betrayed her people at the time of the conquistadors, so the Nicaraguan reader (and others who know the story) may have this resonance of 'betrayal' in mind to contrast with the heroic patriotism of the woman in the poem.

Institutions

Gioconda Belli's poem also offers an example of another cultural matter the translator must consider: feelings associated with institutions. For the Spanish phrase 'hace milicias' translation 1 has 'serves in the militia', translation 2 has 'does her bit in the militia'. Both these translators are British and had the option of translating 'militia' as 'home guard'. This is exactly what it was, a non-professional force to help defend the country against the imminent threat of a US invasion during the eighties, as in the early forties Britain was threatened by a Nazi invasion. It was as ill-equipped as the British home guard during the Second World War, and doubtless Nicaraguans had their jokes about it just as the British did. However, the cultural milieu of Dad's Army would have introduced such a strongly discordant note that neither British translator has risked using the term 'home guard', apparently agreeing it would be disastrous to have echoes of Corporal Jones' shouts of 'Don't panic!' intruding at this point in the poem.

Parts of the Body

Parts of the body also bear different symbolic weight in different cultures. Not all cultures love with the heart. Although we may say 'he's got balls' to mean 'he's brave' in English, this is much more common in a Latin culture with its more bravura machismo. Julio Valle's poem 'Singing a Capture' celebrates the brave revolutionary fighter Doris Tijerino[14] (we quoted Ricardo Morales' poem to her in Chapter 5). The poem is, he says, an apology to her for 'our historical machismo'. As part of his apology he says she is 'con ovarios': 'she's got ovaries'. He means she has been fantastically brave and has the female equivalent of balls. The two words are much closer in Spanish: 'güevos' (balls) means 'eggs'. The image does not work at all in English (especially as, unlike ovaries, womb and cervix are so patently powerful), but then as we read on in the poem we find it must stay because part of her bravery was that the torturers actually ripped open her ovaries and she did not betray her comrades. So the translator was left with a compromise: 'she's got guts, ovaries'. In English 'guts' means courage' but in the New Testament they are the seat of pity. (A modern biblical translator has to be careful not to say someone's 'bowels moved with compassion'.)

Swear Words

Swear words – often related to parts of the body – are also often expressive of a particular culture. 'Puta', a common Spanish swear word meaning 'tart' or 'prostitute' does not translate into English. An equivalent needs to be found. 'Hijueputa' meaning 'prostitute's child' translates into US English as 'son of a bitch', as in the famous saying by President Roosevelt about the dictator Somoza: 'He's a son of a bitch but he's *our* son of a bitch'. But this expression sounds strange in a Cockney or Birmingham accent (or even English R.P.) and a more commonly used English equivalent is probably just 'bastard'. Balls occur again in the last line of the song 'The Strike'[15]:

> ¡y por güevo tiene que amanecer!

(and by ball, dawn has got to break). The English translation has left them out but has tried to provide a substitute with a touch of 'heroic' alliteration:

> one flame is lit, another flame answers . . .
> let's set the darkness on fire
> and damn it, dawn has got to break!

In Chapter 5 we described the poet Leonel Rugama's battle with the National Guard. When the Guard called upon him to surrender he defied them by shouting: 'Que se rinda tu madre!'. Literally this means 'Let your mother surrender!' and is a supreme insult in Nicaragua. If we translate it literally, the reader has to make an imaginative leap into Nicaraguan culture. Because of the difficulty of this, in his translation of Ernesto Cardenal's *Nicaraguan Canto*, Robert Pring-Mill renders the phrase 'SURRENDER? ME? UP YOURS!' Another suggested translation of the exchange is: 'Surrender, you fucker!' 'Fuck off! Fuck your mother!' (This rendering has a British army monotony to it and 'mother' still sounds a bit odd.) The phrase 'Que se rinda tu madre!' uttered by this quiet, clerically educated twenty-year-old poet has become so famous and is so often quoted in Nicaraguan literature that, although it may be somewhat bewildering to the English, there is an argument for translating it literally.

THE WHOLE POEM AS A BODY OF WORDS

We said earlier some translations do not seem to have a substantial body of their own and sound like a ghost of the original. When we say a poem is a body, we mean the whole poem with its own particular shape and physicality. So here is a whole short poem, 'Oscar Turcios'[16] (a Sandinista leader killed at Nandaime in 1973), which has a substantial body and strong clear voice in the original Spanish. Then follows a literal translation, that lacks body and life in English. It is a shadow of its former self. After that comes the the finished translation, which attempts to resurrect the life of the Spanish original.

> Ninguna aristocracia, ninguna
> oligarquía, ningún grupo dominante
> tuvo jamás un club tan exclusivo
> como él de nosotros.
> Para entrar entonces al Frente Sandinista
> había que colgar en la percha la vida
> y yo
> allí la vida les dejé.

Here is a literal English translation:

> No aristocracy, no
> oligarchy, no dominant group
> ever had such an exclusive club
> as our one.
> To enter then the Sandinista Front
> it was necessary to hang the life on a hook
> and I
> left my life there to them.

In this literal 'metaphrase' or crib the English is limp, particularly at the end, which is so simple and powerful in Spanish. Here is an attempt to improve matters:

> No aristocracy, no
> oligarchy, no ruling class
> ever belonged to such an exclusive club
> as we did.
> To get into the Sandinista Front then
> you had to hang your life up
> on the rack and there it was
> that I left mine
> to them for good.

This translation attempts to reproduce the *effect* of the Spanish rhythm. And although they are not present in Spanish, the voiced/voiceless near rhyme club/up, the voiced/voiceless consonant rhyme class/was and the penultimate and final consonant rhymes then/mine, did/good are introduced to give the translation a bit of stiffening and shape, to convey the sense of progression, or even destiny, present in the Spanish original but completely lacking in the English crib. The final pair ending the poem with the line 'to them for *good*' tries to render the epigrammatic, even laconic, solemnity of the Spanish ending, which is helped by the three stressed close front vowels in the last line: *allí, vída* and *dejé*.

For a French example of a translation of a whole poem as a body of words, see Derek Mahon's translation of Philippe Jaccottet below.

TRANSLATIONS OF RILKE

We said earlier that a translation that keeps rigidly to the form of the original may appear dead or forced in English. An example would be this quatrain[17] from a translation of Rilke's *Orpheus Sonnets*:

> Anticipate all farewells, as were they behind you
> now, like the winter going past.
> For through some winter you feel such wintriness bind you,
> your then out-wintering heart will always outlast.

Here are some much better translations of Rilke, which keep close to the original form but to better effect than the previously quoted example. The original of the first verse of 'Narcissus'[18] reads:

Narziss verging. Von seiner Schönheit hob
sich unaufhörlich seines Wesens Nähe,
verdichtet wie der Duft vom Heliotrop.
Ihm aber war gesetzt, das er sich sähe.

Here is a literal translations offering some alternatives:

Narcissus passed / went by / disappeared / vanished. From his
beauty raised itself constant/continuous/perpetual/endless his
essence's / being's closeness / proximity / nearness, thickened /
condensed / compressed like the perfume/fragrance/scent of the
sunflower/heliotrope. To him however it was set (and variants;
n.b. 'Gesetz'= law, commandment), that he should see himself.

Here now is Michael Hamburger's version, which not only keeps the
rhythm and rhyme scheme (with consonant rhyme for lines 1 and 3)
but sounds like a poem in English:

Narcissus perished. From his beauty rose
incessantly the nearness of his being,
like scent of heliotrope that clings and cloys.
But his one avocation was self-seeing.

The first line of Rilke's 'Christ's Descent into Hell' presents a very
tricky problem in the translation of the word 'verlitten':

Endlich verlitten, entging sein Wesen dem schrecklichen
Leibe der Leiden. Oben. Liess ihn.

The word 'verlitten' is the past participle of the verb 'verleiden'
(which is usually used transitively to mean to spoil something for
someone). Here Rilke is using it intransitively in his own way to
mean 'suffer through'. The plain verb 'leiden' means to suffer and
the prefix 'ver' often has a sense of 'away', 'over'. 'Leiden' occurs
as a plural noun in the next line meaning sufferings. Hamburger's
version keeps the German syntax but has had to sacrifice the play
on this word for the sake of rhythm, meaning and resonance:

Beyond it at last, his being escaped from the terrible
body of torments. Above. Left him.

Finally here is a passage from Rilke's 'Turning Point':

Denn des Anschauns, siehe, ist eine Grenze.
Und die geschautere Welt
will in der Liebe gedeihn.
Werk des Gesichts ist getan,
tue nun Herz-Werk

Literally this says:

For, of looking, see, is a /frontier/border/limit.
And the more looked-at/ contemplated world
wants to thrive in love.
Work of sight is done,
do now heart work

Here is Hamburger's version, in which quite small changes make all the difference to the poem's musicality and tone. The use of 'to be nourished by love' works particularly well:

For looking, you see, has a limit.
And the more looked-at world
wants to be nourished by love.
Work of seeing is done,
now practise heart-work

TRANSLATIONS OF APOLLINAIRE

Translating French poetry is notoriously difficult because of its deceptive lucidity. Here are two translations – one by Roger Shattuck [1] and the other by Oliver Bernard (who also did the 'metaphrase' translations in the Penguin Rimbaud) [2]. Each of these translators has rendered the same poem by Apollinaire, keeping closely to the original French form. The French title is 'A La Santé',[19] which is the name of a prison where the poet was sent.
   Part 1 of the poem in French reads:

Avant d'entrer dans ma cellule
Il a fallu me mettre nu
Et quelle voix sinistre ulule
Guillaume qu'es-tu devenu

Le Lazare entrant dans la tombe
Au lieu d'en sortir commit il fit
Adieu adieu chantante ronde
O mes années ô jeunes filles

1.   Before I could enter my cell
        I had to strip to the skin
        A dire voice moaned in my ear
        Guillaume what have you done

        Lazarus thus entering the tomb
        Instead of coming out of it
        Goodbye goodbye the round is sung
        My years and O my pretty girls

2.   Before I got into my cell
        I had to strip my body bare
        I heard an ominous voice say Well
        Guillaume what are you doing here

        Lazarus steps into the ground
        Not out of it as he was bid
        Adieu adieu O singing round
        Of years and girls the life I led

In the second version the rhythm is much better and so is the tone. I particularly like the light touch of 'Well/Guillaume what are you doing here' and the last line ending 'the life I led'. Although this version's rhyme scheme reproduces the French more closely, the language is also closer to the English we speak.

Here are a couple more examples of Oliver Bernard's translations of Apollinaire. The end of the poem 'Fête', which has described a firework display, goes like this:

L'air est plein d'un terrible alcool
Filtré des étoiles mi-closes
Les obus caressent le mol
Parfum nocturne où tu reposes
Mortification des roses

Literally this says:

The air is full of a terrible alcohol/ Filtered by stars half closed/ Shells caress the soft night scent where you rest/ Mortification of the roses.

Here is Oliver Bernard's version. The choice of the word 'liquor' works far better than 'alcohol' and the final couplet neatly solves an extremely tricky problem. The 'false friend' 'mortification' won't do.

> The air is full of a terrible
> Liquor from half-shut stars distilled
> Projectiles stroke the soft nocturnal
> Perfume with your image filled
> Where the roses all are killed

This poem 'La Souris: Mouse' is complete:

> Belles journées, souris du temps,
> vous rongez peu a peu ma vie.
> Dieu! Je vais avoir vingt-huit ans,
> et mal vécus, à mon envie.

Literally this says:

Fine days, mouse (or mice) of time, you gnaw little by little at my life. God! I am going to be twenty eight years old, badly lived ones in my opinion.

Here is Oliver Bernard, once more catching beautifully Apollinaire's wry rueful voice, as in the prison poem. The last two lines of this translation seem to have a totally appropriate echo of Stevie Smith (e.g. in 'The Jungle Husband'). We note his choice of 'mice', presumably because 'days' are plural, although the title of the poem is 'mouse'.

> Beautiful days, time's mice, gnawing
> little by little my life away.
> God! Nearly twenty-eight this spring,
> and misspent years too, I should say.

TRANSLATIONS OF CARDENAL

Here is a last Nicaraguan example giving two translations of part of the same poem. Comparison may bring out some of the problems, which each translator solves a bit differently. One translation is British and one was made in the US.

In the poem 'Elvis'[20] written not long after the Revolution, Ernesto Cardenal – a catholic priest – dreams that Elvis, one of the young members of his community killed in the assault on San Carlos barracks, is taking him to see his new baby:

> la chavalita morenita
> que se te atribuía a vos y era igualita a vos
> y yo te envidiaba por este nuevo hijo,
> porque podías hacer lo que me está negado, porque me lo he
>   negado yo,
> y entonces desperté y recordé que estabas muerto
> y que tu isla Fernando ahora se llama Elvis Chavarría,
> y ya no podías tener ese nuevo hijito que se parecía a vos
> como tampoco yo,
> estabas muerto igual que yo
> aunque estamos vivos los dos.
>
> (80 words)

1. the dark, little girl
    that was said to be yours and looked just like you
    and I envied you for having this new child,
    because you could do what's denied to me, because I have
        denied it to myself,
    and then I awoke and remembered you were dead
    and that Fernando Island is now called Elvis Chavarría
        Island
    and now you couldn't have this new little child who looked
        like you
    just as I couldn't,
    you were dead just like me
    although we're both very much alive.

    (87 words)

2. the dark little girl
    yours and just like you they said

and I envied you this new baby
because you could do what I was denied
although it was self-denial
then I awoke and remembered you are dead
and your isle Fernando is called
Elvis Chavarría now
you can no longer have
that new child to take after you
any more than can I
you are dead like me
although we are both alive.

                                                              (74 words)

Translation 1 uses more words than the original, translation 2 uses fewer. Translation 1 keeps the original line breaks and is closer to the original form and syntax. For example, line 2 describing the dark little girl retains the original indirect speech:

that was said to be yours and looked just like you

whereas 2 changes it into the very words someone might have said:

yours and just like you they said

(This is just the kind of thing people might say in the country in England, maybe in Somerset, but perhaps not in the Mid West?) Does the reader think this change is legitimate? Translation 2 has more sound patterning, some of which is an attempt to echo that of the original. For example, the final rhyme in the original vos/dos (with the two intervening lines ending in 'yo') is echoed by the consonant rhyme have/alive (with intervening lines also ending in vowel sounds). This translation makes quite frequent use of consonant rhyme: said/denied; girl/denial; called/child; have/alive (and often the first of the pair is a short vowel and the second a 'more echoey' long vowel or diphthong). We noted in Chapter 2 that consonant rhyme is often used in English with an elegiac resonance. Again, does the reader think its introduction here is legitimate?

We conclude this chapter with two last examples of poetry translation, one from French and one from German.

TRANSLATION OF PHILIPPE JACCOTTET

The first is Derek Mahon's translation of the complete poem 'Martinets: Swifts' by Philippe Jaccottet:[21]

> Au moment orageux du jour
> au moment hagard de la vie
> ces faucilles au ras de la paille
>
> Tout crie soudain plus haut
> que ne peut gravir l'ouïe
>
> At the stormy moment of dawn
> at the apprehensive time
> these sickles in the corn
>
> Everything suddenly cries higher
> than any ear can climb

There is a question about the choice of 'dawn' to translate 'jour' (literally 'day'). This is a perfectly possible rendering but is it what the original intended? Do swifts cry or sickles harvest at dawn? 'At the apprehensive time' is very good for the difficult French of the next line. 'These sickles in the corn' loses the sense of the swifts 'shaving' the corn. The English sounds good; time/climb is a risky but effective full rhyme echo of the French full rhyme vie/ouïe (although it cannot quite convey the French onomatopoeic rendering of the swifts' shriek). Nevertheless, this is an excellent example of a successful translation of a whole poem as a body of words. Although it does not exactly mimic the original rhythm or rhyme scheme, the English version gives us a very good sense of the French poem *as a body*.

TRANSLATION OF PAUL CELAN

The final example is the end section of Paul Celan's 'Death Fugue' translated by Michael Hamburger.[22] If you read the translation first, it is a very strong poem in English with a substantial English body. (One caution: for the sound the reader needs to know that

Margarete is pronounced with four syllables, roughly: Mar-gar-et-er: /mɑːɡaretə/.) Then read the German and you find the English is miraculously close to it in rhythm, sound, feeling, meaning. We feel the poem's 'Germanic' quality but the language is absolutely English. However, look again and you will see that the translation is not an artless literal rendering. For example, lines 5 and 6 have a strong rhyme in German blau/genau. Literally they read:

> death is a master from Germany his eye is blue
> he hits you with lead bullet, he hits you exactly/precisely

Hamburger reproduces the German's strong rhyme and introduces several other modifications to make his version correspond, apparently so effortlessly, with the original:

> death is a master from Germany his eyes are blue
> he strikes you with leaden bullets his aim is true

'Be it observed that I include in the meaning of a word not only its correspondent object but likewise all the associations which it recalls.' I think Coleridge would have been impressed by this translation:

> Schwarze Milch der Frühe wir trinken dich nachts
> wir trinken dich mittags der Tod ist ein Meister aus Deutsch-
> 	land
> wir trinken dich abends und morgens wir trinken und trinken
> der Tod ist ein Meister aus Deutschland sein Auge ist blau
> er trifft dich mit bleierner Kugel er trifft dich genau
> ein Mann wohnt im Haus dein goldenes Haar Margarete
> er hetzt seine Rüden auf uns er schenkt uns ein Grab in
> 	der Luft
> er spielt mit den Schlangen und träumet der Tod ist ein
> 	Meister
> aus Deutschland

> dein Goldenes Haar Margarete
> dein aschenes Haar Sulamith

> Black milk of daybreak we drink you at night
> we drink you at noon death is a master from Germany

we drink you at sundown and in the morning we drink and
    we drink you
death is a master from Germany his eyes are blue
he strikes you with leaden bullets his aim is true
a man lives in the house your golden hair Margarete
he sets his pack on to us he grants us a grave in the air
he plays with the serpents and daydreams death is a master
    from Germany

your golden hair Margarete
your ashen hair Shulamith

NOTES

1.   Derek Walcott, *Omeros* (London: Faber and Faber 1990).
2.   *Spleen* translated by Nicholas Moore (London: Menard Press, 1990).
3.   'Psalm 57' (58 in RSV) by Ernesto Cardenal is translated in *Nicaraguan New Time*.
4.   Nuala Ní Dhomhnaill, *Pharaoh's Daughter* (Oldcastle: Gallery Books, 1990).
5.   Cf. the famous repetition of the words *'the same'*, *'the same'*, *'the same'* in the definition of the Council of Chalcedon (451) on the two natures 'in one person and subsistence' of the incarnate word. Denziger, *Enchridion Symbolorum* (Freiburg: Herder, 1946).
6.   'El Cristo de Palacagüina' song by Carlos Mejía Godoy is on the cassette *Cantos de la Lucha Sandinista*, II (imported by Nicaragua Solidarity Campaign).
7.   *Nicaraguan Mass.* Cassette with bi-lingual text translated by D. L. published by Catholic Institute for Internaltional Relations (London, 1986).
8.   'El chocoyito' by Irene Agudelo in *Poesía campesina de Solentiname* (Managua 1980).
9.   'Night' by Pedro Pablo Meneses translated by Peter Wright is in *The Peasant Poets of Solentiname*. For other ingenious translations of onomatapoeic bird language, see Robert Pring-Mill's translation of Ernesto Cardenal's *Nicaraguan Canto*, final section, in *Zero Hour and other Documentary Poems*.
10.   Augustine of Hippo, *Confessions* XII, 16, 23.
11.   'Nueva Ecología' and 'Meditación en un DC-3' by Ernesto Cardenal are in *Vuelos de Victoria*, translation by D. L. in *Nicaraguan New Time*.
12.   'St Pancras Lock' by D. L. in *St Pancras Wells* (London: Hearing Eye, 1991).

13.   'Nicaragua agua fuego' by Gioconda Belli is in *De la costilla de Eva*. The translator of 1 is John Lyons in *Nicaragua Water Fire* (Warwick: Greville Press Pamphlet, 1989); the translator of 2 is D. L.

14.   'Singing a Capture' by Julio Valle-Castillo is in *The Nicaraguan Epic*.

15.   The song 'The Strike' is part of the 'Canto Epico to the FSLN' in *The Nicaragua Epic*.

16.   'Oscar Turcios' by Julio Valle-Castillo is in *The Nicaraguan Epic*.

17.   From *Sonnets to Orpheus* II, 13, translated by J. B. Leishman (London: Hogarth Press, 1957).

18.   'Narcissus', 'Christ's Descent into Hell' and 'Turning Point' are all in *An Unofficial Rilke*, bi-lingual text translated by Michael Hamburger (London: Anvil, 1981).

19.   Guillaume Apollinaire, 'A la Santé' is in *Selected Writings of Guillaume Apollinaire*, bi-lingual text translated by Roger Shattuck (New York: New Directions, 1971) and *Apollinaire Selected Poems*, bi-lingual text translated by Oliver Bernard (London: Anvil, 1986). Bernard's translations of 'Fête' and 'La Souris' are also in this volume.

20.   'Elvis' is in *Vuelos de Victoria*. The translator of 1 is Marc Zimmerman in *Flights of Victory* (New York: Curbstone Press, 1988). The translator of 2 is D. L. in *Nicaraguan New Time*.

21.   'Martinets' ('Swifts') by Philippe Jaccotet is in *Philippe Jaccotet Selected Poems* translated by Derek Mahon (London: Penguin, 1988).

22.   'Todesfuge' ('Death Fugue') by Paul Celan is in *Paul Celan Selected Poems*, translated by Michael Hamburger (London: Penguin, 1990).

Conclusion

There is no conclusion. Poetry is a wording of life. We live for a number of years, life goes on. Poetry is a necessity and a grace, an abundance of life. We take part by hearing and speaking, reading and writing it, by making it, doing it here and now. The poetry of the past still lives in us when we incorporate it into our lives. We try to share the poetry of other cultures by learning other languages or through translations. All this enriches the life, the poetry, where we are here and now. That being said, nothing is more deadening than sitting through an evening of bad poetry. It arouses frustration and ill humour and fights may break out in the pub afterwards.

There is no exclusion. Poetry is not for an 'elite' few but for anyone alive who can speak a language and is willing to serve an apprenticeship. 'For every man whose soul is not a clod hath visions and would speak if he had loved and been well nurtured in his mother tongue.' Or woman, of course. Poetry is the most language of language. Through language we shape ourselves and our world. Poetry is the most incarnate of language. Word embodied, set up among us and we have seen its glory.

So the final note is practical. There is poetry going on all over the country. I apologise if the following examples seem London-based. This is because that is where I live and is certainly not meant to suggest that poetry is confined to London. A little research should turn up what is available in your area and the post still works (some of the time). Many of the most vigorous small poetry presses are not London-based. There is also a certain amount of poetry on the radio. You could look in *Radio Times* both for the programmes and to note which programmes invite poems to be sent in.

If you possibly can, visit the excellent Poetry Library in the Festival Hall on the South Bank of the Thames. This stocks a huge range of contemporary English poetry and poetry in translation. It also has cassettes and magazines. It is free. It publishes lists of poetry groups in the London area, countrywide lists of bookshops stocking a good range of poetry, poetry magazines, poetry publishers, festivals and so on. If you cannot visit the library, the librarian will send these lists to you. The quarterly *Poetry London Newsletter* publishes details of poetry activities in the London boroughs. For other areas you could try your regional arts board (for lists, even possible funding), local library or paper. If you want to join a poetry group, you could check out a few until you find one that suits you. Perhaps you might also investigate your local adult education institute. Poetry workshops or groups may put on readings and produce a pamphlet or anthology of the group's work.

There are all kinds of venues which put on poetry readings. Some of them regularly have 'poets from the floor'. Most regular venues will publish a leaflet of their programme and some will have a mailing list (e.g. the Voice Box next to the Poetry Library in the Festival Hall). Poetry events in London are listed weekly in *City Limits* and *Time Out*. If you are putting on an event yourself, these listings are free but you need to check in the magazine for their copy deadlines. Local papers such as the *Camden New Journal* and the *Ham and High* also have free listings. You could check your own local papers.

There are numerous small magazines. These can be found in some libraries and bookshops. In London, as well as the Poetry Library, the University Library in the Senate House stocks a number of poetry magazines and if you can get a ticket it is pleasant to spend an afternoon browsing there. The University College London Small Press Collection is open to the public. Local libraries may stock local poetry magazines. As many magazines run on a very tight budget, you may want to subscribe to one or more. If you want to submit poetry to a magazine, be sure to read at least a couple of copies of it first to get a feel of what the editor publishes.

Certain bookshops have a better poetry stock than others (see Poetry Library list and investigate your area). Sometimes bookshops put on poetry events. The intermittent and completely independent publication *Poetry Listing* edited by David Hart gives an excellent survey of what poetry has been published during a given period.

When you have a collection of poems you may want to try a book publisher. You probably have a better chance if you have already published poems in a number of small magazines. As well as the Poetry Library's list, there is a list of poetry publishers (and other useful lists) in Macmillan's *Writer's Handbook* and the *Writer's and Artist's Yearbook*. Do not get depressed if you keep getting rejections. These publishers can only publish a very small amount of the poetry being produced and each editor will have individual preferences. It is essential to the health of English poetry that what is published is not confined to the taste of a few individual editors.

The Association of Little Presses and the Small Press Group each publish a yearly handbook listing member presses and some of their publications. You could try sending your work to some of these small presses. You will note that many of them are run by people who publish their own work. With the current state of technology this is often a feasible option. Many prefer it because they can control their own production. The problem of course will be distribution. However, if you look round bookshops you will find that poetry books published even by quite large publishers are not particularly well distributed either.

Local arts boards may be able to help with funding for publications or events. The Arts Council of Great Britain has a limited number of Writer's Bursaries, a translation fund and other schemes. They publish their funding guidelines every year.

These are just a few ideas about of where to look for poetry in Britain. If you investigate you will find others. Poetry is essential to the life of any society. If you have a contribution to make as listener or speaker, reader or writer, you are more than welcome, you are needed. However, every would-be poet takes an enormous risk. What is needed is good poetry. Ah, you reply, but who is to say what is good poetry? To that question this book has not tried to propose any final answer, merely to make a few suggestions.

Short List of Addresses and Publications

The Poetry Library, South Bank Centre, London SE1 8XX (071 921 0664/0943) stocks a very large range of contemporary poetry and poetry in translation, cassettes, magazines etc. Membership is free. Up to four books at a time may be borrowed. Also publishes many useful lists of poetry groups, festivals, magazines, publishers, bookshops etc.

Arts Councils
The Arts Council of Great Britain, Literature Department, 14 Great Peter Street, London SW1P 3NQ (071 333 0100) has some funding for poetry, a limited number of Writers' Bursaries, a translation fund etc. Write for their Literature Funding Guidelines.

Scottish Arts Council, 12 Manor Place, Edinurgh EH3 7DD (031 226 6051).
Welsh Arts Council, Museum Place, Cardiff CF1 3NX, Wales (0222 394711).

Arts Council of Norther Ireland, 181a Stranmillis Road, Belfast BT9 5DU (0232 381591).

The Arts Council, 70 Merrion Square, Dublin 2, Eire (010 3531 611840).

Regional Arts Boards
Write to the Literature Officer in your area for further information.

Eastern Arts Board, Cherry Hinton Hall, Cherry Hinton Road, Cambridge CB1 4DW (0223 215355).

East Midlands Arts Board, Mountfields House, Forest Road, Loughborough, Leicestershire LE11 3HU (0509 218292).

London Arts Board, Elme House, 133 Long Acre, Covent Garden, London WC2 9AF (071 240 1313).

Northern Arts Board, 10 Osborne Terrace, Newcastle-upon-Tyne, NE32 1NZ (091 281 6334).

North West Arts Board, 12 Harter Street, Manchester M1 6HY (061 228 3062).

Southern Arts Board, 19 St Clements Street, Winchester SO23 9DQ (0962 855099).

South East Arts Board, 10 Mount Ephraim, Tunbridge Wells, Kent TN4 8AS (0892 515210).

South West Arts Board, Bradninch Place, Gandy Street, Exeter EX4 3LS (0392 218188).

West Midlands Arts Board, 82 Granville Street, Birmingham B1 2LH (021 631 3121).

Yorkshire and Humberside Arts Board, 21 Bond Street, Dewsbury WF13 1AX (0924 455555).

*

Poetry Listing lists all poetry published in the last few months. Woodwind Publications, 42 All Saints Road, Kings Heath, Birmingham B14 7LL (021 443 2495).

Poetry London Newletter, Persiflage Press, 26 Clacton Road, London E17 8AR (071 520 6693) lists poetry groups, events and other poetry news for the London area, borough by borough.

City Limits, 66/67 Wells Street, London W1P 3RB (071 636 4444) has a weekly poetry listing column. If you wish to insert a listing of a poetry event, this is free but be sure to meet their deadline.

Time Out, Tower House, Southampton Street, London WC2 (071 836 4100) also has a free weekly poetry listing column.

Small Press Yearbook, Small Press Group, BM BOZO, London WC1 3XX (0234 211606) lists all member small presses and their recent publications.

Catalogue of Little Press Books in Print published yearly by Association of Little Presses, 89a Petherton Road, London N5 2QT (071 226 2657).

The Writer's Handbook, annual publication edited by Barry Turner, published by Macmillan/PEN, lists publishers, magazines, organisations of interest to poets, Arts Councils and Regional Arts Boards and much other useful information.

The Writer's and Artist's Yearbook (London: A. and C. Black) also has useful lists and information.

The Poetry Society is now at 22 Betterton Street, London WC2H 9BU (071 240 4810).

*

Longman Pronunciation Dictionary by J. C. Wells (Harlow: Longman, 1990).

The Rhythms of English Poetry by Derek Attridge (Harlow: Longman, 1982).

Metre, Rhyme and Free Verse by G. Fraser (London: Methuen, 1970).

An Introduction to the Pronunciation of English, by A. C. Gimson, Fourth Edition revised by Susan Ramsaran (London: Edward Arnold, 4th edn, 1989).

Phonetics by J. D. O'Connor (London: Penguin, 1973).

The Poet's Manual and Rhyming Dictionary, Frances Stillman (London: Thames and Hudson, 1966).

How Poetry Works by Philip David Roberts (London: Penguin, 1986).

A Dictionary of Literary Terms by Martin Gray (Harlow: Longman, 1984).

The Concise Oxford Dictionary of Literary Terms by Chris Baldick (Oxford: Oxford University Press, 1990).

A Dictionary of Literary Terms by J. A. Cudden (Harmondsworth: Penguin, 1976).

A Linguistic Guide to English Poetry by Geoffrey N. Leech (Harlow: Longman, 1969).

The Ideology of the Text by Christopher Hampton (Buckingham: Open University Press, 1990).

Index